Defeat At Sea

Defeat At Sea

The Struggle and Eventual Destruction
of the German Navy, 1939–1945

by C. D. Bekker

Illustrated with Photographs

New York   Henry Holt and Company

Around the northernmost tip of Jutland a cruiser squadron is steaming at high speed into the North Sea. They make a magnificent sight—these four powerful warships with the white mustaches of the bow waves beneath their noses. A beautiful but at the same time a sad sight, for here is all that is left of the major war vessels of the German *Kriegsmarine*— all that is left after five and a half years of war against a superior enemy—the heavy cruiser *Prinz Eugen* and the light cruiser *Nürnberg*. It is May, 1945, a few days after the German surrender. This last passage by German warships is being made under "escort" of two British cruisers from Copenhagen to Wilhelmshaven. And scarcely has the squadron turned into the North Sea when the British senior officer's ship, the *Dido*, makes the signal to part company: *Prinz Eugen* and *Nürnberg* are to proceed to Wilhelmshaven—and into captivity.

Suddenly, as the ships are closest to one another, a signalman climbs out onto the wing of the Englishmen's bridge—"*Commanding Officer to Commanding Officer*," he makes. Not dozens but hundreds of pairs of German eyes are fixed tensely on the semaphore flags, and hundreds of rough seamen's voices laboriously repeat letter after letter in low tones as they read the last message from the enemy, the good wishes of a victor for the vanquished: *Auf Wiedersehen—until—better—days.*

All of them realize that this message is more than a polite gesture. It reveals something of that chivalrous spirit which, with very few exceptions, has animated their tough but fair sea adversary all through the period of merciless "total" war.

When the German officer to whom this signal from the Englishman was addressed related this occurrence to me, I was only at the start of my researches into the fate of the *Kriegsmarine*. That was a long while back. It was certainly no light task that I had taken on. For in 1945 only a few documents remained in German hands about the five and a half years which had gone by. In the interval the English had, it is true, published a whole series of important documents taken from the files of the German Naval Staff. And these, together with other papers which I had at my disposal, could have sufficed for an unambitious historian; but for me, who wished to paint a colorful picture of the war at sea which would grip the reader, they were but the necessary rib framework which as yet lacked flesh and blood.

In the meantime I have visited hundreds of former members of the *Kriegsmarine*, of all grades from admirals to ordinary seamen, who had personal experience of the decisive hours of their service. I found the greatest willingness to help me to the best of their knowledge. But I also heard a number of skeptical opinions: the dramatic events of the war at sea had been described too often in sensational but untruthful fashion.

The publication in serial form of my book in the *Illustrierte Woche* has caused even these skeptics to change their opinion. Apart from this it has brought me a flood of correspondence from readers, from former members of the *Kriegsmarine* who were able to confirm the facts described from their own experience as well as from some who passed me new material or who corrected this or that error of detail. All of this has placed me in a position to produce this first edition of the book in an improved, enlarged, and corrected form.

I wish particularly at this point to thank all those who have helped me in seeking out all the innumerable details which have been recorded in this book. They number so many that it is impossible for me to make my acknowledgments to them by name. But my special thanks are due to Admiral Theodor Krancke and Konteradmiral Gerhard Wagner, who by reason of their all-embracing knowledge of the events described have watched over the historical accuracy of the whole.

C. D. BEKKER

Publishers' Note

THAT THIS BOOK, WHOSE AUTHOR SERVED IN THE LAST war in the German Navy until the was taken prisoner by the British in 1944, may be read as presenting the war at sea from 1939–45 as seen through German eyes is substantiated by the following statements by two outstanding German admirals:

This work reproduces the actual course of events of the war at sea in the form of episodes, but nevertheless in objective and truthful fashion. Among other appointments during the war, I was captain of the armored ship *Admiral Scheer*, Admiral-Quartermaster, for one year representative of the Commander in Chief of the Navy at the Führer's headquarters, and Commander in Chief of Gruppe West. The manuscript was submitted to me for correction, in order that I could pick out any inaccuracies. Insofar as I am able to judge, and making allowance for minor journalistic license, the volume can be looked upon as authentic throughout.

Theodor Krancke, Admiral a.D., Düsseldorf

In order to prevent the intrusion of inaccuracies into this work I undertook, at the request of the German publisher, to correct the manuscript from the point of view of historical accuracy before it went to press. By his most careful regard for the truth of his facts the author has succeeded in putting together a gripping and lifelike account which will appeal to expert and layman alike, and constitute a proper memorial to the struggle of the German Navy.

Gerhard Wagner, Konteradmiral a.D., Bremen

During the whole war Konteradmiral Wagner was one of the leading officers of the German Naval Staff. From 1941 to 1944 he was Chief of the Operations Division of the Naval Staff. After the war he was for nearly four years a member of the Naval Historical Team formed by the U.S. Navy.

Contents

1

The Beginning and the End

Oₙₗy A WEEK TO CHRISTMAS, THE FESTIVAL OF PEACE —Christmas, 1945. True, the war is over, but it's going to be a sad festival all the same. Millions of Germans are longing to go home, no matter how desolate their homes have become. But instead . . .

A long column of British army trucks is winding its way through the streets of Wilhelmshaven, between mounds of debris, every truck crammed with Germans in navy blue uniforms. Alert, the ratings' suspicious eyes never leave the British guards and their machine guns. None of them knows where they are going. Two days ago they were taken off their ships, where the reduced crews were still carrying out their duties. Nearly all that was left of the German Navy has been concentrated by the English in Wilhelmshaven, where the men have been since May; now it is nearly Christmastime, and neither officers nor men have the faintest idea what the victors intend doing with them.

Toward the end of August they had heard rumors that the "Big Three" had divided the remaining vessels of the fleet among themselves at Potsdam, but up to now nothing had happened.

The endless waiting was getting the sailors down. What if they were to be handed over to the Russians?

"In that case you can count me out," most of them said.

Week after week went by—then suddenly, two days ago, they had been transferred to the Mühlenweg barracks. The British had brought up entire companies, sealing off the dockyards where the ships lay, bringing machine guns into position and even driving up with tanks. Did they suspect something? Nobody knew the answer.

Now they had once again been bundled into army trucks guarded by British soldiers. Captain Giessler, the German officer commanding the cruiser *Nürnberg*, was being driven in an English car at the head of the convoy. As much in the dark as the others, he watched the road attentively, hoping to discover where they were going. Then he recognized the road to the harbor—so they were going aboard again! As the car swung round the last turning, there was the *Nürnberg* lying in her usual berth—but there was something else as well.

A Russian sentry was posted on the gangway, Russian soldiers were lined in front of the ship. In a flash the captain understood: his beautiful ship was to be handed over to the Russians; the rumors had been true. The crew had been taken on this two-day "excursion" so as to allow the Russians to examine her thoroughly for any signs of "sabotage." The sentries, the tanks, and the machine guns had been brought up to prevent his men from taking French leave when they realized they were sailing to Russia.

It was obvious the Russians could not take the *Nürnberg* safely out of the harbor on their own. That was why they were bringing the German crew along. But what guarantee was there that it would ever be allowed to come back?

A single Englishman, Captain Conder, was waiting on the deck. Now, walking up to the German commander, he proceeded to read out an official British statement:

"This ship is no longer a German ship. It is now a unit of the Soviet Navy. In future you will take your orders from the Russian captain commanding the cruiser. I remind you in your own interests that this vessel represents an important contribution to Germany's reparations. If it should not be handed over in good condition, the consequences for Germany would be most unfortunate. All of you must understand this. You will accordingly take your ship to a Russian port. . . ."

In the meantime the trucks had drawn up on the pier. By now every man realized what was happening; even the youngest midshipman had recognized the Russians' impassive faces. "I only hope the men won't do anything foolish before I have a chance of speaking to them," Giessler was thinking. "Things are going to get warmer one way or the other in any case. Unless the English give us pretty binding guarantees, at least half the crew will have disappeared for good before we're halfway through the Kaiser Wilhelm Canal. . . ."

Captain Conder was still reading his statement: "I know you are afraid you may never return"—the faces of the Russian officers standing round remained expressionless—"and that this fear may cause you to act in an unreasonable manner. But I can assure you that you are mistaken. Vice-Admiral Levchenko has given my Commander in Chief his word of honor that every man who does not volunteer for further service on the cruiser will be brought back safely to Wilhelmshaven. After that, when it has been ascertained that you have not committed any acts of sabotage, you will be demobilized from here. In the meantime, do your duty. . . ."

Sabotage—there was nothing the Russians feared more, and on this voyage it was to be Bugbear Number One.

As soon as the British captain had finished, the senior Russian officer present also read a declaration, in which the Germans were asked to behave loyally and similarly warned against committing acts of sabotage. The text contained these words, translated liberally:

"I guarantee good treatment at the hands of the Soviet crew, good food, and a return home for all German officers and seamen."

Both declarations were handed to Captain Giessler. But could he trust these two paper promises? Were the Germans not completely defenseless, deprived of all rights? Who would move a finger for them if the Russians held them back against their will?

The crew had lined up on the quarter-deck, waiting with set faces to hear what their captain had to tell them. It was not going to be easy, anything but easy!

"A British detachment will accompany you to Lepaya and will then escort you and your crew back to Wilhelmshaven," the Englishman added.

Splendid, here was something Giessler could tell his men!

Shortly after Christmas the Red admiral, who spoke fluent German, moved into his cabin on board the *Nürnberg*. The Germans found that they got on better with the Russians than they had expected, but the Allies did not seem to hit it off at all. The Russians wanted to seize as much material as they could in Wilhelmshaven, but the British refused to let anything go. The Germans tried to keep out of the dispute, but it was not always possible.

In the meantime the sailors had resigned themselves to the inevitable. They were prepared to take their ship to Lepaya . . . after all, the British were escorting them, and the Red admiral had given his word of honor! The Russians, meanwhile, never ceased stressing the fact that the sole responsibility for bringing the cruiser to her destination lay with Germans.

The *Nürnberg* started on her last voyage on January 2, 1946, a destroyer, two torpedo boats, and the ancient target ship *Hessen* with her small wireless-control ship *Blitz* steaming in the same convoy toward their new employment. By January 5 they were approaching Lepaya—and not a single act of sabotage had been committed.

Nevertheless, the Russians had some very anxious hours ahead of them. The Soviet High Command had decided that the *Nürnberg* was to lie at anchor in the roads of Lepaya. This order was certainly not intended for bad weather, and above all not the

heavy swell there was that evening. It would be madness to anchor; the cables would be bound to snap. Though the Russian
officers realized this, they could do nothing about it. Instead they
shrugged their shoulders with the comment, "Orders are orders."

"Then we must get new ones. Haven't we got an admiral on
board?"

But even the Red admiral was powerless against "orders," so
the ship was anchored after all. Half an hour later the heavy
cables had indeed snapped and the anchors were lost.

What now? It was well into the night, and it was impossible
to tow the ship through the narrow canal to Lepaya until next
morning. Squalls of rain reduced visibility to nil, and there were
no beacons. Besides, the mine fields had not been swept yet. The
Russians didn't like the look of it at all.

"What shall we do now?" the Red admiral asked.

"Steam up and down all night," Giessler told him, "and fix
our position by radio."

"Impossible!" several of the Russian officers shouted, trying
to dissuade their admiral. "It's sabotage! Position by radio? It
can't be done!"

"If the German captain says it can be done," he roared back
at them, "it will be done. Do you understand?"

Accordingly, all night long, they navigated by radio beam,
with the Russians watching like lynxes. If something went wrong
now, in sight of their own port, the consequences would be pretty
nasty. However, Captain Giessler and his crew navigated by
radio as happily as a man rides a bicycle on a 60-foot paved road.
They had done it before in 1941, when they were operating
with the *Scharnhorst* and the *Gneisenau* in the Atlantic; it was
just part of the day's work for them. Still, the Russians kept shaking in their shoes in case something happened, and only breathed
again when dawn broke.

Tugs came alongside, but the hawsers parted.

"We'll show these fellows where they get off and bring her
in under her own steam," Giessler decided.

A risky business, through the narrow, tubelike, winding

Lepaya canal! But already the order had come through to all stations:

"Ship will enter harbor without tugs."

Every seaman knew that everything now depended on the quickest possible reactions on the part of each individual. The *Nürnberg* was 600 feet long, with high freeboard which caused her to blow badly to leeward in the stiff breeze. Nevertheless, the difficult maneuver succeeded. The Russians did not say a word. Now all that remained to be done was to turn the ship at an angle of 90 degrees in the inner harbor, and then go stern first to her berth.

At this moment the last shots of this war were fired by Germans in Soviet Russia. They were pistol shots, and they were fired on January 6, 1946, falling straight into the crowd on the pier below which had been watching the ship's maneuvers in openmouthed astonishment—a crowd of sailors, workmen, and spectators. They scattered like the wind and took cover.

For a space a deathly silence reigned on board the *Nürnberg* —then a great roar of laughter went up, in which even the officers on the bridge could hardly refrain from joining.

These last shots of the war had been fired from line-throwing pistols. The German seamen had shot across the first line for making fast the ship onto the jetty, but the jetty was now deserted. Evidently this method of shooting lines to the jetty was still unknown here. In the end a cutter had to be lowered to bring back the lines that had floated away. It was quite a little time before the pier was once more crowded by Russian soldiers.

General satisfaction reigned on the bridge, the Germans because the maneuver had succeeded, the Russians because they had brought the ship back without sabotage. The Red admiral was trying to find the right words. He turned to the German captain, saluted, and said with a sigh of relief:

"No Russian officer could have carried out that maneuver."

"You would have managed it, Admiral, I'm sure."

The Russian shook his head dubiously and murmured, "H'm . . . maybe . . . maybe."

His officers stood round impassively, not having understood a word.

"Three cheers for the good old *Nürnberg!* Hurray, hurray, *hurray!*"

So, eight months after the end of the war, some with tears in their eyes and others biting their lips, the German crew took leave of their ship, far from home, in a Soviet port. Nobody interfered with them. All round lay Russian vessels, their crews watching curiously from the decks, and the jetty crowded with sight-seers. As the Germans gave their three resounding cheers, even some of the Russian officers saluted.

Both Russians and British kept their word: the crews of the ships that had been handed over left Lepaya in the submarine tender *Otto Wünsche,* set for home. The *Nürnberg,* back in the inner harbor, slowly disappeared from sight. She is the only "big" ship of the German Navy still afloat today. She has been renamed *Admiral Makarow* and belongs to the Russian Baltic fleet. The heavy cruiser *Prinz Eugen,* which also survived the war, has been lying at the bottom of the Pacific near the coral reefs of the Bikini atoll since 1946. The Americans had secured her in Potsdam in order to use her as a target ship for their atom-bomb experiments. The aircraft carrier *Graf Zeppelin* and the pocket battleship *Lützow* fell into the hands of the Russians, the one unfinished and the other heavily damaged, but it is not known whether they have repaired them and incorporated them into their fleet.

That was the end of the fleet with which Germany set out to oppose England in 1939—a single cruiser left, and that under the Soviet flag. But did anyone really believe that the end would be different? Can anyone in the German Navy have earlier contemplated a renewed naval war against Great Britain at that particular time with confidence?

The facts themselves provide the answer to these questions. Germany and England reached an agreement on June 18, 1935, whereby both powers agreed that the German Navy might reach

35 per cent of the strength of the Royal Navy. This also applied to individual types of ships such as battleships, cruisers, destroyers, etc. Germany was permitted to construct U boats up to 45 per cent, after 1938 even 100 per cent of the British submarine tonnage. This had apparently been the first step toward an Anglo-German understanding, whereby Germany recognized Britain's hegemony on the sea. The naval rivalry between the two countries which had existed up to the First World War seemed now to have been done away with. The naval pact might have been the foundation of genuine peace.

On July 15, 1935, Admiral Erich Raeder, C.-in-C. of the Navy, issued a secret order to his officers in which he said: "The agreement arises out of our decision to exclude forever the possibility of Germany and England becoming enemies. . . ."

Four years later things took a different turn. Hitler was dazzled by his early successes in Austria and Czechoslovakia, and expected from England a "weak acquiescence" to his further plans. In a speech made to his generals and admirals on August 22, 1939, at Obersalzberg, in which he set out his plans to attack Poland, he said:

"England's position is much too precarious. I accordingly believe it impossible that a responsible English statesman, given this situation, should incur the risk of a war."

If this was intended to calm the Navy's fears, it hardly succeeded. Take Commodore Dönitz, for instance. He was in U boats as a young officer in the First World War. In 1935, after the signing of the Naval Agreement, he got his first three U boats, the nucleus of the *Weddingen* flotilla; after that he became head of the U boat arm with the job of teaching his commanders how to move the things, to dive, and to fire. But by August, 1939, he hadn't really got very much further, with precisely 22 boats that could be put into action in the Atlantic. This is as much as to say—since it is a matter of experience that two thirds of available boats are always either in port, on the way to their objectives, or returning from them—that at most seven boats at a time could be used against Britain. Obviously these would not be enough for the conduct of a war.[1]

As regards battleships, cruisers, and aircraft carriers, Germany's situation was even worse, her construction plan being calculated to cover at least ten years, and now being only in the first stages. In time a fleet could be built, composed of traditional types in appropriate numerical relationship, to serve the purpose of safeguarding Germany's maritime interests and increasing her value as an ally. This "homogeneous" fleet, which in percentage terms would always be much smaller than the British, clearly showed in its construction that it was never intended for a war against England. It might, of course, have been possible to build more U boats—the most appropriate type of weapon for use against the British—while the construction of other types was correspondingly held back. But it was precisely in the case of U boats that the circumstances did not exist for which the Naval Agreement provided. So now the decision of a war against England depended on the armament manufacturers.

On September 3, 1939, at noon the C.-in-C. U boats was standing in his chart room looking at a large map showing the positions of his boats. Eighteen were at sea, 18 in all. . . . It would be madness to think of inflicting serious damage on the enemy with these few boats in the event of a war with England. Pinpricks, that was all they could achieve. Anxiety was written in the lines on Dönitz's forehead. Two days earlier he had sent his last urgent memorandum, stressing the need for developing U boat strength, to the OKM—the Supreme Naval Command.[2]

The door was flung open and an intelligence officer entered hastily. "Sir, a signal from the OKM!"

It was the British declaration of war.

Dönitz threw back his head, clutched the fatal scrap of paper,

---

[1] In September, 1939, Germany had fifty-seven U boats in all. But twenty-four were too small for Atlantic service, and eleven were still being rebuilt.

[2] OKM—*Oberkommando der Kriegsmarine.*

and crumpled it as he gave audible vent to his exasperation. Then, his arms akimbo, he swung round, strode into his room, and locked the door.

The officers of his staff waited for half an hour before Dönitz reappeared. His face still showed traces of his agitation, but he gave his orders in cool, measured tones.

The Battle of the Atlantic had begun.

That afternoon, September 3, 1939, a conference was held at the headquarters of the Supreme Command of the German Navy, the OKM, in Berlin on the conduct of operations at sea. After the daily over-all reports on the situation the "Chief," Grossadmiral Raeder, remarked casually, "Gentlemen—the small circle, please!"

This meant that the most important decisions would now be taken in the presence of only a few officers. Most of those present rose quickly to their feet and took their leave with a short bow. A little while later those who remained were gathered round the table: the supreme commander, the Chief of Staff for naval operations, Admiral Schniewind, the chief of the operational division, Admiral Fricke, his deputy, Fregattenkapitän Wagner, and the head of Raeder's personal staff, Fregattenkapitän Schulte-Mönting.

"Gentlemen," Raeder began in his lively way, "today war against England and France has broken out, although the Führer, to whom I expressed my misgivings, had assured me repeatedly that the Navy need not consider this eventuality before 1944." The Chief hesitated for a second or two—the only sign that betrayed his emotion. Then, firmly, he began drawing the consequences of the new situation, hard but inevitable as they were. The young navy was composed of new ships all right, but they were hardly more than a sample of what should be still to come. With little battle experience and few heavy units, it was an embryo only—utterly out of keeping with what any Naval Command, traditionally understood, should have at its disposal.

Later it was frequently said that Raeder cared only for his "big" ships, his battleships and cruisers, but had no use for the

U boat arm, while Dönitz had no use for anything but it. That neither was true is shown for the first time quite clearly by the grave decisions of September 3, 1939.

"We cannot even think of attacking the British fleet, much less of destroying it," Raeder said. "Consequently, we must concentrate on harrying the enemy's merchant navy, and the most promising weapon for that purpose is the U boat. What we need is U boats, and still more U boats!"

This decision, taken by Grossadmiral Raeder as unhesitatingly as any responsible man would have done in his place, was not in any way due to the influence of the U boat commander, Admiral Dönitz. The latter had merely sent the following memorandum to Berlin:

"With 22 boats and a prospective increase of one to two boats a month I am incapable of undertaking efficacious measures against England." [3]

He had made his meaning clear. His C.-in-C. replied immediately that he was giving orders to the Department of Naval Construction to work out a new plan of U boat construction, so that 20 to 30 new boats a month might be sent on operations. Naturally this could only be done at the expense of the rest of the shipbuilding program, and forgoing the construction of new battleships, aircraft carriers, and cruisers. This was perfectly well known to Raeder, the creator of the new German fleet, and possibly it hurt him, but on September 3, 1939, his decision stood firm—U boats were what he must have.

Two to three years later the Battle of the Atlantic, as the English called it, was approaching its climax. Would the German U boats, which in June, 1940, had had an increase rate of three and in October, 1941, of 23 a month, succeed in wresting the hegemony of the seas from Britain? That would be a decisive blow against the latter's war potential, separated as she was from American power reservoir by the Atlantic and with her absolute need of sufficient transport tonnage.

---

[3] See note on page 19.

In the summer of 1942 the Germans were sinking shipping representing over a million tons' loading capacity a month, while replacements, although, especially in America, they were being built at feverish speed, managed to total no more than just half that amount. For June, 1942, alone the British Admiralty reported the loss of 145 merchant ships, some of which carried extremely valuable cargoes.

However, while the Germans threw more and more U boats into the battle and kept working out new tactics to break into enemy convoys, their opponents were naturally also increasing and improving their methods of defense. The graph of U boat sinkings was rising, gradually but consistently. Up to August 24, 1942, 105 had failed to return, out of a total of 304 in action since the outbreak of war. Some commanders made port successfully six, seven, eight times over. But fate caught up with them in the end . . . it was a merciless fight, and all our victories were balanced out by painful losses.

In August, 1942, 12 boats failed to return. Losses had never been as high before. These were difficult days for those surrounding Admiral Karl Dönitz. And the enemy defense was becoming stronger and stronger.

The reasons for the increasing success of the Allies' defensive tactics lay in the consolidation of their security system, which made it more and more difficult for German submarines to break through the multiple lines of escorting destroyers to attack the convoys. Above all they were to be found in the tremendous increase of that most dangerous enemy of the U boat —aircraft with superior speed. The area over which this deadly weapon could operate was spreading out further and further from the shores of the British Isles, from Ireland, Greenland, and North America. The U boats were being driven out from the land masses, where they were no longer safe, further and further into the open sea, where aircraft could not pursue them—*not yet.*

At the Nürnberg trial in 1946, Admiral of the Fleet Dönitz said with reference to that period of the war:

"The standard by which it must be judged was the ubiquitous and continually sharper watch kept by the huge British and American air forces. Though at that time I had reached the apogee of my success, this was a problem which worried me extremely, seeing that starting from the summer of 1942 our U boat losses from bombing from the air rose suddenly, if I remember rightly, by more than 300 per cent."

2

The Sinking of the *Laconia*

"YOU SEE WHAT I AM SUGGESTING, DEFENDANT, IS THAT the statement, the warning, that you would sink merchant ships, if armed, made no difference to the practice you had already adopted of sinking unarmed ships without warning."

These words were spoken by Sir David Maxwell Fyfe, the Deputy British Chief Prosecutor at Nürnberg. At that time he had been cross-examining Dönitz for days on end in a duel as hard fought and exciting as scarcely any other before the bar of this court. For the last Chief of Naval Staff, who only a short time before the end of the war had ordered that the daily records of the war at sea were not to be destroyed, as the Navy had nothing to hide, it was a life-and-death duel.

When many months later judgment was passed, the Allied judges acquitted Dönitz of the first point of the accusation (conspiracy of crime against peace), but condemned him to ten years' imprisonment in respect of points 2 and 3 of the accusation (conducting a war of aggression and offenses against the laws of warfare). In its summing up the court said among other things:

"Although Dönitz built and trained the German U boat arm, the evidence does not show that he was privy to the conspiracy to wage aggressive wars or that he prepared and initiated such wars. He was a line officer performing strictly tactical duties. . . . It is clear that his U boats, few in number at the time, were fully prepared to wage war. . . . The real damage to the enemy was done almost exclusively by his submarines, as the millions of tons of Allied and neutral shipping sunk will testify. . . . In the view of the Tribunal, the evidence shows that Dönitz was active in waging aggressive war."

As special grounds for the condemnation the court gave the following: (1) After he had become Commander in Chief of the Navy Dönitz did not, as far as his command was concerned, cancel Hitler's "Commando Order" of October 18, 1942, which, contrary to international law, directed that commando and sabotage troops taken prisoner were to be executed. (2) Dönitz in his position unquestionably must have known that inhabitants from the occupied countries were being held in great numbers as prisoners in the concentration camps. (3) At a conference with Hitler and Jodl in February, 1945, as to the advantages and disadvantages of giving notice of withdrawal from the Geneva Convention, Dönitz expressed the opinion that "It would be better to carry out the measures considered necessary without warning, and at all costs to save face with the outer world."

A special role in the case against Dönitz was played by the accusation that the German U boat war was contrary to international law and, therefore, criminal. As one of the principal proofs Sir David Maxwell Fyfe brought forward the order given by Dönitz after the *Laconia* incident, which was conveyed by radio on September 17, 1942, to U boat commanders on the oceans of the world.

No attempt is to be made to save members of sunk ships.

How did this order come to be given? What had happened in those September days in the middle of the Atlantic, about 500 miles south of the Azores?

Around midday on September 12, 1942, *U 156*, with Kapitänleutnant Hartenstein in command, is working slowly toward the calculated "rendezvous" with the enemy. This is a fast single-decker. And, sure enough, before long a short promenade deck can be made out, the unmistakable sign of a ship which is half freight and half passenger steamer.

"I estimate it to be about 6000 tons gross, Herr Kaleu."

"Somewhat bigger, I think—let's say 7000 to 8000. Shortly after it begins to get dark we shall be close enough."

At 9:00 P.M. *U 156* comes up for the surface night attack. A salvo of two torpedoes leave tubes 1 and 3. In about two minutes they must detonate if they hit at all. . . .

There is hardly anyone on the bridge who does not look at his watch. Two minutes. The men stand motionless. Two minutes ten seconds. Any second now the impact must come—but still there's nothing. Two minutes thirty seconds. Somebody shakes his watch. Heads are twitching nervously. Two minutes fifty seconds!

The commander bites his lips. Through the night glass he can see the enemy before him as if on a salver as tranquilly the ship goes on its way, the white foam of its bow wave standing out clear. For several minutes now she hasn't been zigzagging, so it can't be because of that. By now the tin fish have been running more than three minutes. They're sure to have crossed long ago. . . .

With an angry shrug of his shoulders Hartenstein puts the glass aside. To have missed at the ridiculous range of 1500 meters!

At that precise moment a flash shoots up in the distance, and another. For fractions of seconds the steamer has burst into blazing light. Two hits! The dull roar of the detonations comes rumbling over the sea.

Everybody is now waiting expectantly for news from the wireless office. After a few moments the operator raises his hand.

"She's sending out an SOS on 600 meters!"

SOS — SOS — Laconia torpedoed — Laconia torpedoed — SOS. . . .

Laconia?

Feverishly hands turn over the leaves of the list of ships—there it is: *Laconia*, Cunard White Star Line, Liverpool, 19,695 gross registered tons.

So that is the solution of the riddle, a 20,000-tonner!

"You see," the commander grins, "my estimate was nearest!"

The *Laconia* has got a severe list; boats are being let down into the water. As *U 156* goes cautiously closer, its crew can make out in front the first castaways.

"*Amico—amico!*" they're shouting. Italians apparently.

As the first one is pulled up on the deck, a Mediterranean-shaped head and a tattered Italian uniform emerge. There is no doubt about it.

"Are there more Italians?"

The man brandishes his arms in the air and won't stop talking. Thousands of comrades, he says. Meanwhile the German sailors are pulling up more people onto the U boat deck, including, at last, one who can speak a few words of German, from whom they learn more. On board the transport *Laconia* there were between 1400 and 1800 Italian prisoners of war. Allegedly the Poles on guard did not open the prisoners' quarters after the torpedoes had hit, and most of the prisoners had tried to squeeze themselves through the portholes to get out of the sinking ship.

U 156 has now fished up nearly 100 men, among them some Englishmen.

The *Laconia* had a crew of 463 on board, with a further 268 men on their way to England on leave, besides 80 women and children. One by one, 22 lifeboats can be made out, but not how many people there are floating about in the water and crying for help.

In the night of September 12–13 the following radio message was received at U boat headquarters in France:

Sunk by Hartenstein British Laconia, square 7721. Unfortunately with 1500 Italian prisoners. Up to present 90 picked up. Request orders.

The officer on duty at once woke the Chief. Two minutes later Admiral Dönitz was standing in front of his map studying the position. Radio messages shot out one after the other—the Admiral was giving orders to U boats in the vicinity.

Schacht—Polar-bear Group—Würdemann—Wilamowitz proceed forthwith to Hartenstein, square 7721, help picking up survivors. Maximum speed!

Meanwhile Hartenstein's U boat lay in the midst of the wreckage of the sunken transport. Wherever the eye fell there were swarms of shipwrecked people swimming in the water, the German sailors indefatigably dragging out anyone they could catch hold of. The whole night long it went on and into the next day, but even after a few hours the U boat was overcrowded. With an additional 193 men on board, there was no room to sit down, or even to move; in every nook and corner of the boat human beings were squeezed against each other like herrings in a cask. If the U boat had to make an emergency dive now it would mean catastrophe. Nevertheless, still more people were clamoring to come on board, and just could not understand that they could be refused. The Germans kept on trying to help those still swimming around by distributing them among the nearest lifeboats.

Admiral Dönitz was greatly concerned when he learned by radio of this development. Nobody knew better than he what danger he was sending his U boats into here. In saving the shipwrecked they must inevitably neglect their own safety. What was going to happen if enemy naval forces or, still worse, enemy bombers suddenly came on the scene? And that was only too probable, in view of the messages the *Laconia* had sent. . . .

Warning after warning now went out:

Safety of U boats not to be endangered in any circumstances. Boats must at all times be ready for emergency dive. Keep a good lookout for enemy aircraft and submarines. All boats, including Hartenstein's, are to take on board only as many people as consistent with boat being fully maneuverable after diving.

Meanwhile U boat Command in France had arranged with the French Admiralty that a light cruiser and other fast French ships should sail from Bingerville and Dakar to take over the rescue work and so release the U boats.

Each of three German U boats, *156*, *506*, and *507*, was now crammed full of survivors and in addition had four or five overcrowded lifeboats in tow. In this way they held their course slowly toward the rendezvous agreed with the French. Since the morning after the *Laconia* went down Hartenstein had been sending out every few hours, on the international 25- and 600-meter bands, plain language messages in English.

Any ship that will come to the assistance of the Laconia's *crew will not be attacked by me, provided I am myself not attacked by ships or aircraft. German U boat.*

One steamer which, to judge by the strength of its signals, must have been standing quite close at hand did not react. On the other hand, numerous Allied shore radio stations repeated the message, including an American airfield on the West African coast.

At 11:25 A.M. on September 16, 1942, four days after the sinking, *U 156* had just succeeded in collecting its four lifeboats together again after they had been scattered during the night when the towline parted. Suddenly a lookout on the bridge shouted:

"Aircraft bearing 70 degrees!"

The general automatic reaction was to make for the conning-tower hatch—get below and dive! But there was nothing to be done about it with the lifeboats hanging on the towline, the decks uncleared, and below still over 100 Italians and English officers, women, and children.

But the commander had already provided for this kind of eventuality.

"Bring up the Red Cross flag!"

Six-foot square, it had been sewed together by the crew, and six men now spread it aloft and held it toward the enemy as the heavy four-motor Liberator with American identification marks came roaring up. This instant would decide whether they were going to drop their depth charges—hundreds of human beings in *U 156* and in the lifeboats gazed intensely upward and held their breath. Now they would be coming . . . now . . . too late! The Liberator zooms away over the U boat, alters course, reduces height—and comes in again as before.

At that moment an Englishman approaches the German commander on the bridge, an officer of the R.A.F. who had been on his way home on leave.

"Look here, sir," he says, pointing to the visual-signaling gear, then to himself, then to the aircraft, "I could talk with him in our language, with our signs and abbreviations. . . ."

For a moment Hartenstein hesitates. Then he orders the lamp to be switched on.

"All right! You will tell me beforehand what you want to signal," and so saying he turns to the Englishman and gives him the lamp.

It is one of the strangest, most exciting moments of the war at sea. A British officer held prisoner is signaling in Morse code from a German U boat to the American bomber ready to let loose death and destruction on all on board, whether they be friend or foe: Englishmen, Germans, Poles, Italians—men, women, and children.

At first the American pilot does not react, but keeps on flying up and circling round. The Englishman explains what the position is, inquires after ships in the proximity which could take the people who have been picked up—but still the American does not react. The other doesn't lose heart, but again signals: *On board this U boat there are English people from the* Laconia, *soldiers, civilians, women, children.* . . . Again there is no reply.

The bomber goes away, flies as far as visibility distance, returns, goes away again. Half an hour later it is back again—or is it another one? In any case it's a bomber of the same type, a Liberator. The machine comes flying at a height of between 2000 and 3000 feet—everybody's staring upward wondering if it'll give a signal now. Yes, indeed, here it comes!

Two depth charges, just ahead of the U boat. So that's it! Several soldiers on deck get splinter wounds.

"Cut the tow!" Hartenstein shouts.

Here's the Liberator roaring back again from astern and slinging its next charge right among the *Laconia* lifeboats. One of them gets a direct hit and capsizes—dozens of English and Italians sink in the water.

The next two depth charges detonate with a delay of a few seconds directly below the control room of *U 156*. The boat rears up, gives a bound, and falls back deep into the sea, the conning tower disappearing for a few seconds in a black swirl of water, the Red Cross flag hanging in tatters on the guardrail. From the control room and the bow compartment it is reported that water is coming in.

"Ready with life jackets! All English and Italians overboard!"

But the boat's still floating, still functioning, the engines still running! They can even get their noncombatants to the lifeboats and clear them off there. The Liberator has flown off again. . . .

"I'm fed up with saving people," Hartenstein curses, as he makes his way from the scene, submerged. The damage is less than at first appeared: periscope, diesel, battery cells, wireless mast, hydrophones—all are damaged. But they will probably be able to repair it all fairly well themselves—somewhere quietly at sea. It is a wonder *U 156* is still afloat and can still move and dive.

"I knew it!" Dönitz blurted. "It just couldn't work!"

The OKM had just rung up to say that Hitler did not want

U boats to be endangered through rescue work, and now that was just what had happened. The discussion at OKM headquarters was loud and heated.

"We rescue the enemy and while we do it he kills us," a young officer observed bitterly. "I propose, Herr Admiral, that all survivors from this moment on be left to their fate." That meant those who were still in the other U boats, endangering them exactly as *U 156* was endangered.

"I cannot just let them be thrown back into the water," Dönitz retorted. "The lifeboats are all overcrowded."

"But if something nasty happens again . . ."

"Then we'll be there—and there'll be more lifesaving! But tomorrow the French will be there too, and the trouble will be over in any case." The Admiral took a deep breath. Then, banging on the table, "But I tell you this," he declared; "from now on it's finished. The time is over when we could do as we liked on the surface. From now on I forbid it. The enemy air arm is superior to ours, and ubiquitous. The risks we have been taking are simply in plain contradiction to the bald logic of things. The use of the Red Cross flag has not been provided for, consequently it has no effect on the Americans."

The next morning, June 17, a second German U boat engaged in rescuing survivors had bombs dropped on it, though here again the result was not too bad. But Dönitz's patience was at an end, and the order went out by radio:

Acceptance of any forbearance on the part of the enemy toward U boats on account of rescue operations is completely incorrect. Then followed the order forbidding rescue work once and for all.

Four years later, in the summing up of the International Military Court at Nürnberg after a description of the development of the U boat war and British countermeasures, it was declared that by reason of the facts adduced the Court could not declare Dönitz guilty for his conduct of the U boat war against armed British merchant ships. On the other hand, giving notice of operation zones and sinking neutral merchant ships in those zones without giving them warning was an offense against the London Protocol of 1936. With regard to the *Laconia* order the Tribunal was of opinion "that the evidence does not establish with the certainty required that Dönitz deliberately ordered the killing of shipwrecked survivors. The orders were undoubtedly ambiguous, and deserve the strongest censure. . . . In view of all the facts proved and in particular of an order of the British Admiralty announced on May 8, 1940, according to which all vessels should be sunk at sight in the Skagerrak, and the answers to interrogatories by Admiral Nimitz stating that unrestricted submarine warfare was carried on by the United States from the first day that nation entered the war, the sentence of Dönitz is not assessed on the ground of his breaches of the international law of submarine warfare."

Today hundreds of English people who were then on the *Laconia* are still alive, for of 811 English almost 800 were saved, while of 1800 Italians only about 500 got away with their lives. The three U boats which achieved this rescue operation were all destroyed by bombing during their next sorties against the enemy.

The *Bismarck*

Four long years the imperial german high seas Fleet during the First World War—with the exception of a few operations only, of which one led to the Battle of Jutland—was kept in harbor on the basis of false strategic assumptions. The consummation of this strategy was that its sailors turned revolutionaries and the idea became established that the High Seas Fleet had been afraid to show up in action. This unjustified imputation continued to influence the conduct of leading German naval officers until September, 1939, when the few units of the young German Navy again found themselves up against the world's greatest sea power. Here and there the fear was gaining expression that this war too would probably be over without the Navy having achieved anything. It was natural its slogan now should be, "Don't let us be too careful this time!"

Strategic considerations must be the governing factor in deciding whether to risk one or the other of the big ships in the vast extent of the Atlantic. The enemy's arteries must be cut. Thus to sink merchant ships, transports, and reinforcements, and then to disappear as fast as possible so as not to be caught by superior British naval forces—that was the task.

In this way the "hit-and-run" tactics were born, the tactics of the German "ghost ships": fast, secret, always appearing suddenly just where they are not expected, they sink their ship and vanish again into the ocean. Eel-like, they slip away as soon as things get a bit hot, and of course they maintain the strictest radio silence. The magic radar screen which later on will reveal to the English what cannot be seen with the naked eye does not yet exist, while air reconnaissance is still in its infancy. How in these circumstances can the "ghost ships" ever be caught?

The early successes of these operations exceeded even the most sanguine expectations. The three "pocket battleships" *Deutschland, Admiral Scheer,* and *Admiral Graf Spee,* the heavy cruiser *Admiral Hipper,* and auxiliary cruisers in their pursuit of enemy merchantmen sent hundreds of thousands of tons of valuable cargo to the bottom the four seas over.

At the beginning of 1941 the two battle cruisers *Scharnhorst* and *Gneisenau* put out to the Atlantic and in operations lasting two months sank 22 ships aggregating 115,622 gross registered tons. At the Admiralty in London the atmosphere was electric. The way these "ghost ships" kept vanishing into thin air and yet apparently always had enough fuel to turn up somewhere else seemed the devil's own work.

By this time it had become a matter of course for German naval officers to operate with their *Seetakt* radar-ranging apparatus, while the enemy radar was still limping far behind. The Germans still had the lead in this field, and could still play "cat and mouse" with the enemy. At OKM headquarters on the Tirpitzufer in Berlin, however, they had no illusions. The C.-in-C. of the Navy knew quite as well as his admirals and staff officers that the English were doing everything they could to put an end to this game. The sooner the battleships put out again the better the prospects of being once more successful with "hit and run." A new armored colossus had just ended its trial runs in the Baltic Sea: the 41,000-ton battleship *Bismarck,* while its sister ship *Tirpitz* would be ready a few months later. That was at least something to carry on with.

The *Bismarck* was to undertake its first sortie against the enemy in company with the *Scharnhorst* and the *Gneisenau* which were lying ready at Brest. Action must be fast, fast! But there was bad news coming in from Paris: the *Scharnhorst* had damage to its engines, while the *Gneisenau* had been hit several times by the indefatigable attacks of British torpedo and bomber aircraft. The repair work was bound to go on until the summer.

Grossadmiral Raeder had to make a difficult decision—and time was pressing. The *Bismarck* must go out alone, accompanied only by a heavy cruiser, the *Prinz Eugen.* Yet to send a single battleship almost alone into the lion's den, into the Atlantic, where the English were burning to wipe out the scores of the last few months, was more than ordinary daring.

"Ought we not, Herr Grossadmiral, to put the operation off until at least the *Scharnhorst's* engines are in working order? By that time, moreover, the *Tirpitz* will have completed its working-up exercises."

It was Admiral Lütjens who made this suggestion on his departure from Berlin. As it was his flag which would be flying in the *Bismarck,* he didn't think the recklessness of his superior very clever.

But the Grossadmiral was influenced by other problems. In the Mediterranean the German attack on Crete was impending, and the English must be prevented from strengthening their Mediterranean fleet. The same applied to the reinforcements for North Africa—urgently required by Rommel. The only way to attain the desired end was to threaten the British Atlantic lines with German naval forces. Thus Raeder had weighty grounds for sticking to his decision.

"But by then, my dear Lütjens, it'll be summer, and we should have to write off any chance of a break-through into the Atlantic passing unnoticed." Lütjens had a mind to reply, "That's as may be." At any rate that was his conviction, though he couldn't say so, as he himself was to lead the expedition. It might look as though he had cold feet.

"Who knows whether in two or three months we shall still be putting to sea at all, Lütjens? There just is no other choice: the *Bismarck* and the *Prinz Eugen* must put out alone. . . ."

This first and last operation of the German flagship, which on the evening of May 21, 1941, set out from Bergen on its fatal six days' journey, was fuller of incredible occurrences, of confusions, strange chances, false assumptions, success, and tragedy for both adversaries, mad as they were to get at each other, than almost any other naval operation of such short duration can have been in the whole history of war at sea.

Since May 20 the Commander in Chief of the British Home Fleet, Admiral Sir John Tovey, in his flagship at Scapa Flow, had been in the greatest anxiety—air reconnaissance and agents in Denmark had discovered that the *Bismarck* and the *Prinz Eugen* were on their way northward. What could they want in Norway? Probably nothing else than a break-through from there into the Atlantic—the standard pattern. And on the twenty-second a reconnaissance report confirmed this: the berth in the Grimstadfjord near Bergen, in which the German ships had been lying the previous day, was empty.

The operation with the code name *Rheinübung* (Rhine exercise) had begun. Sir John Tovey did not hesitate a moment to issue his orders. He stationed cruisers at all the passages leading into the Atlantic and despite the miserable weather ordered air reconnaissance flights in the hope of locating the Germans. To the Denmark Strait, between Greenland and Iceland, he sent the cruisers *Norfolk* and *Suffolk* with the new radar apparatus, which certainly ought to catch the *Bismarck* despite the fog and mist which at this time of the year lay above the edge of the pack ice.

Meanwhile Vice-Admiral Holland was lurking south of Iceland with the battle cruiser *Hood*, the biggest warship in the world, and the 35,000-ton battleship *Prince of Wales*, which had just been put into service. The Commander in Chief himself sailed with his flagship *King George V*, the battle cruiser *Repulse*, the aircraft carrier *Victorious*, and four more cruisers.

The whole afternoon of May 23 the *Suffolk* and the *Norfolk* were taking advantage of the veil of fog and mist spread wide over Iceland's north coast. However, about eight o'clock that evening a sailor on the *Suffolk* suddenly made out the German ships. Captain Ellis immediately turned around and pointed his bows toward the *Bismarck,* so as to get the latter within the arc of his radar apparatus, with which he could only operate ahead. With excitement he followed the two bright pips on the light screen: the Germans all right! Slowly the pips wandered over the screen; the ships were now steaming outside the fog and passing the lurking British cruiser. The latter would not lose touch with them again until her own battleships were brought up.

At the same time Sir John received the comforting report:

We have found them!

Quietly the British squadron steamed toward the spot where it estimated it would meet the enemy. The *Bismarck* was not going to escape.

But there were still going to be a good many surprises. . . .

The first and—for the English—the most painful surprise took place in the early daylight of May 24. At 5:50 A.M. Vice-Admiral Holland with the *Hood* and the *Prince of Wales* trained his guns on the Germans and opened fire.

Admiral Lütjens on the *Bismarck* had the order to avoid as far as possible any encounters with superior or equal forces and to confine himself to his principal task of upsetting the enemy lines of communication across the Atlantic. If, however, a fight was unavoidable, then he should fight with all the means at his disposal.

In Lütjens' opinion it would be impossible to shake them off, with the same radar-ranging apparatus on board as his own, perhaps even better; accordingly, he gave orders to go into action. The effect of the firing took everyone's breath away as the two German ships concentrated their aim on the *Hood.* After exactly six minutes a towering sheet of flame shot up out of the 46,000-ton warship, and just after that the whole ship was surrounded with a wreath of yellow and red leaping flames, a mushroom of black smoke spreading wildly out above it. A huge block of white-hot metal burst up, to sink hissing back into the sea—that must have been one of the heavy gun turrets. The *Hood* had received a direct hit in its after magazine—the *Hood* was blowing up.

Shift target to the left! the order went through the German ships. Most of the men still could not comprehend their magnificent success. Ten minutes later the *Prince of Wales* had also been severely hit several times and turned away under dense black smoke.

The whole fight had lasted only 24 minutes. The *Prinz Eugen* was unharmed; the *Bismarck* had received two hits from the *Prince of Wales*, was losing some oil, and must reduce speed. But what was that compared with the great success—one battle cruiser sunk, one battleship hit seven times and badly damaged!

And yet its own hits did weigh heavily on the *Bismarck*, enough to prevent it from carrying out its proper task. First and foremost, with a trail of oil visible from the air from a considerable distance, it was impossible to play "ghost ship" in the Atlantic without being picked up. Quite apart from that, Admiral Lütjens did not believe he would be able to escape the British cruisers which were still keeping in touch by means of radar.

From the English point of view, after their heavy initial losses it had become urgent to bring up superior naval forces to put an end to the *Bismarck*.

Under cover of a rainstorm it proved possible to detach the *Prinz Eugen* unnoticed into the Atlantic for commerce raiding. The *Bismarck* was now alone, and must inevitably draw the pack of hounds onto itself if it were to try to reach the French coast by making a sweep around the British Isles.

Wherever in the Atlantic there were British warships for the protection of convoys or other tasks, they were now ordered up by the Commander in Chief. Two other battleships, the *Ramillies* and the *Rodney*, were taking part in the hunt. The *Bismarck* was being encircled! Even from Gibraltar, Force H—the battle cruiser *Renown*, aircraft carrier *Ark Royal*, and cruiser *Sheffield* —was putting to sea under Admiral Somerville in order to close the ring from the south. It was, in effect, these last which were later on to play a decisive role when the *Bismarck* had broken through almost as far as the French coast.

For the present the *Suffolk* and the *Norfolk* were still shadowing the ship, keeping in touch by means of their radar. The German Admiral was growing desperate. With her new radar search receiver the *Bismarck* could receive the pulses of the enemy radar, and Lütjens knew, therefore, at every minute that the Englishman was holding him firmly on a bridle—or so he thought. . . .

Just that, however, was his great mistake.

How he made it is simple enough to explain. The English cruisers sent out high-frequency pulses, which were reflected from the steel body of the *Bismarck* and again caught at the point of departure. In this way the German ship would appear as a pip or point on the screen of the British radar. At that time, however, the range of this new and as yet not completely developed technical marvel was only about 13 kilometers.[1]

The German radar search receiver on board the *Bismarck* showed the enemy's radar transmissions. Since it only received, it had a much larger range than the British radar, as it did not need the energy to send out strong pulses of its own. The British radar needed a degree of energy sufficient for the double journey, there and back. The German search receiver, however, picked up the pulses after they had made only the one journey.

It thus came about that Lütjens believed himself inescapably caught in the clutches of the enemy radar because he was always picking up enemy pulses. He could not know that these pulses no longer had the strength to be reflected back to the English. He did not in fact know that since 3:00 A.M. on May 25 his pursuers had lost touch, in a word, that he had escaped from them.

Meanwhile at the Admiralty in London and on Sir John Tovey's flagship there was consternation—the German ghost ship had indeed disappeared! The only thing to be done now was to continue the search further toward the southeast in the supposition that the *Bismarck* was aiming to put into Brest.

---

[1] A considerable underestimate. [Publishers' note.]

Yet just at this point numerous Allied shore radio stations simultaneously reported that a German ship in the sea area in question had just sent out two long radio messages. That could only be the *Bismarck*. Had the Germans gone mad? Now, when they could quietly disappear, when the whole British fleet was nervously—and aimlessly—groping around for them, here they were suddenly writing an account of themselves in the air, so that even the most blundering radio operator could pick it up. It didn't seem possible.

And yet it was so. This time the consternation was in Berlin and in Paris at Gruppe West. There, by observation of enemy radio communications, the *Bismarck's* escape from the shadowing of the British radar had been noted. Just now, nevertheless, here was Lütjens transmitting long radio signals!

Yet it was in these messages themselves that the explanation was to be found. Lütjens felt himself being continually dogged by radar. Therefore, since the enemy already knew where the *Bismarck* was, he might just as well send out his good news and describe his victorious fight with the *Hood*. . . . Back came an urgent signal from Paris telling him for heaven's sake to keep silent and that the English had lost touch long ago.

But it was by now too late. Several Allied shore radio stations had already picked up the *Bismarck*—the bearings had only to be plotted on the chart—and the position of the ghost ship was again known. For the sake of speed the Admiralty sent the bearings by radio direct to Sir John in the *King George V* for his officers to work out the position for themselves.

Sir John Tovey was extremely astonished when his officers handed him the result of the plotting of the bearings with the *Bismarck's* position. From there it appeared the Germans were far away to the north; they must have turned on their tracks and be planning to get back again through the Denmark Strait. And he had thought they wanted to put into Brest! Rapidly adapting himself to the new situation, Sir John gave orders to turn back.

Yet from that moment on what he had previously feared was to take place: he was really proceeding at full speed in the wrong direction. In practice, the *Bismarck,* as before, was holding to its course toward France without ever having had the slightest intention of steaming back northward.

Exactly nine hours later the British noticed that they had plotted the bearings wrong. The supposed northerly position of the *Bismarck* was a mistake by the staff officer in the *King George V* who actually plotted them. In reality the *Bismarck* was standing on hundreds of miles farther to the south.

Sir John Tovey shook his head as now for the second time that day he gave the order: *Reverse course!* But this time the *Bismarck* had such a start that only by a miracle now would it be possible to intercept it. The "miracle" was the Force H of Admiral Somerville, to which the aircraft carrier *Ark Royal* belonged and which for the last few days had been coming up at full speed from Gibraltar.

Still trying to puzzle out where the *Bismarck* had disappeared to, for the last 31 hours the British had been groping in the dark. And hour for hour the German flagship with giant strides was no doubt getting nearer and nearer safety.

At 10:30 A.M. on May 26 came the redeeming signal through the air: by chance, through a break in the clouds, a Catalina flying boat had seen the German ship beneath it—and at once been smothered with antiaircraft fire. Riddled like a sieve, it had just been able to get home. But that brief glance had been enough—the *Bismarck* had been found again!

Hurriedly the British staff officers made their calculations, cheered by a new hope—Force H was not far away! If the Catalina had not come in with its fortunate discovery, the German ship would have virtually jumped the last hurdle. The *Renown,* the *Ark Royal,* and the *Sheffield* were at once put onto a parallel course. At the same time a signal went over from London to Admiral Somerville not to go into action alone but to wait till other battleships had come up. Clearly the British did not want to risk losing another capital ship. But these other battleships were lying far astern, beaten in the race. . . . Therefore the job was to try by all means to reduce the enemy's speed.

The only way of doing that was by torpedo attacks. The sea was stormy, the deck of the aircraft carrier dancing up and down like a man possessed. Nevertheless the Swordfish torpedo aircraft must take off somehow, and at 3:40 P.M. they did leave for the attack. Low over the angry sea they come flying along toward the ship, release their torpedoes, wonder a moment why the *Bismarck's* formidable antiaircraft fire has not yet reached them, increase height . . .

And then, horrified, they see it is the British cruiser *Sheffield* toward which their deadly torpedoes are now worming their bubbly way—though five of them, it is true, have exploded as they struck the crests of the waves. Wildly curving, the cruiser struggles to get out of the way of the others—and succeeds!

But the Englishmen's last hope of stopping the *Bismarck* would seem to have gone.

Nevertheless, there shall be one more, one absolutely last, chance. Four hours later the torpedo aircraft take off again, and this time they find the right enemy, dive down into the German antiaircraft fire, drop their torpedoes—and hit. One of the torpedoes crashes against the side armor of the colossus. The ship shudders a little—that's all. But a second hits it not more than a yard from the rudder, utterly smashing everything that enables the ship to be steered. Rudderless, the *Bismarck* can no longer maneuver, can only turn around in a circle. Here, almost at the edge of the radius of action of its own air arm, it has received this mortal blow.

So Sir John Tovey, who was about to give up the chase for lack of fuel, was the victor after all, and could now bring up his battleships and destroy the giant. On this same evening of May 26 Lieutenant Wohlfarth, commander of *U 556,* suddenly saw the *King George V* and *Ark Royal* steaming toward him. By radio signals he had been informed of the death struggle of the *Bismarck*—instructions had gone out from U boat headquarters to all nearby boats to proceed to her help if at all possible. But in this raging sea the submarine failed to reach the enemy. By chance the two English ships were steaming directly in front of the tubes of *U 556*. In his war diary Wohlfarth wrote:

"I do not even have to move up any more, I am exactly in the right position for attacking. The enemy is without destroyer protection and is not zigzagging. I am lying between the two ships and could dispose of both of them at one and the same moment . . . if I only still had some torpedoes! Perhaps I could have helped the *Bismarck*."

But *U 556* was on its way back from other operations, and had shot them all.

So was consummated the fate of the German flagship *Bismarck*. Rudderless, completely torn to pieces after a two hours' bombardment by a superior enemy, it sank in raging seas at 10:40 A.M. on May 27, 1941, though not without inflicting heavy damage on the enemy, which cost two British battleships many months of repairs in a United States dockyard. The *Bismarck* went under after its commander, Captain Lindemann, had given his last order to scuttle the floating wreck. With the *Bismarck* went 1900 Germans, including Admiral Lütjens, to a sailor's death. Eight battleships, two aircraft carriers, four heavy and seven light cruisers, 21 destroyers, six submarines, and far more than a hundred aircraft were assigned by the British Admiralty to attain this end.

Sir John Tovey has written that the *Bismarck* fought an exceedingly gallant fight against a superior enemy and sank with its flag flying.

4

Running the Gantlet

IN GERMANY WIDE DEPRESSION REIGNED OVER THE LOSS of the flagship *Bismarck*. Hitler summoned Grossadmiral Raeder to Obersalzberg and demanded an account of his supposed tactical errors.

"Why did Lütjens not turn back when he had sunk the *Hood?*" the Führer asked furiously. "Why did he not go after the *Prince of Wales* when it was badly hit? To sink two battleships at a single stroke would have been a really amazing victory. By such means the *Bismarck* would have achieved an aura of invincibility . . ."

Would have . . . if only . . . such arguments were repugnant to Raeder. Anyone would find it easy to win battles and even wars back here at home behind a green table. He, Erich Raeder, knew that a ship had to be commanded from its bridge. The commander of his flotilla had been a capable and gallant officer, to whom he could and indeed must entrust the ship. The fact that fate had caught up with them both was a thing with which he, as Chief of Naval Staff, had always had to reckon, ever since his hit-and-run tactics he had begun the game of putting salt on his mighty opponent's tail.

As it was, with one blow the hitherto successful system of Germany's ghost ships had collapsed. Once the *Prinz Eugen* had broken through the British blockade and reached Brest safely, a few days after the loss of the *Bismarck*, headquarters waited in vain for good news from their supply ships. The British had caught them out; they had discovered the secret of the ghost ships and turned the discovery to their own advantage.

In deepest secrecy the OKM had built up a network of these supply ships and tankers in remote, unfrequented parts of the Atlantic, so that a German battleship operating on the open seas was always sure of being able to stock up with supplies and oil. Now the British had suddenly called the bluff—in the course of a large-scale search six of the seven supply ships had fallen into their hands. The experiences of the *Bismarck* had also shown only too plainly that the enemy was rapidly progressing in two other spheres, the first that of radar, the second the expanding activity of their air force which was gaining control over ever-greater sea areas. All this did not encourage hopes for new successes with the ghost ships. The fact had to be faced: the German Navy could no longer count on using large ships in the Atlantic. The brunt of the attack on England's lifeline had to be increasingly borne by U boats, which Germany did not possess in anything like sufficient number.

Meanwhile the *Scharnhorst* and *Gneisenau* were still lying in Brest harbor, where they had been joined by the *Prinz Eugen*. But what use were they there, seeing that they could no longer be sent out into the Atlantic? Night after night the R.A.F. attacked them with bombs and torpedoes, and it was surprising that the damage was not greater. On top of all this, orders had come from Hitler's headquarters to the OKM that in no case were these heavy ships to be exposed unnecessarily to further risks. The loss of the *Bismarck* had been a severe blow to the dictator, who was especially sensitive to losses of prestige, and extremely proud of his battleships. The order was to avoid all risks, a restriction which Raeder tried again and again, but vainly, to have countermanded.

In any case it was obvious that the ships had to be removed from the hail of British bombs in Brest, where during the last eight months the R.A.F. had dropped 4000 tons of high explosives.

One day a whisper went round the staff of the 2nd Security Division in Boulogne to the effect that the "old man" had gone temporarily off his head. Today, February 12, 1942, at noon, he had suddenly and without a word of explanation ordered all available officers and men of his command into cars and army trucks, and was leading the convoy up onto the heights of Cape Gris-Nez.

"Now, gentlemen, at ease," chuckled Captain von Blanc, one of the few officers who were in on the secret; "we just wanted to let you have a look at the sea."

The men felt like schoolboys being taken on an excursion. What were they supposed to see here? Doubtful glances followed the captain, who was walking up and down agitatedly. A coxswain saluted:

"Sir, may I ask what . . . ?"

That was as far as he got. The officer thrust a pair of binoculars into his hand and, swiveling him round by the shoulders, pointed to sea in a southwesterly direction. Neither the coxswain nor any of the others were ever to forget what they then saw.

Down there to the left, just below the coastline, a squadron of ships was steaming at full speed—five, eight, 15 battleships large and small—a whole fleet! In the center three big ones—beyond doubt the battle cruisers *Scharnhorst* and *Gneisenau,* as well as the *Prinz Eugen.* Surrounded by destroyers, torpedo boats, and E boats, the unit was approaching at high speed, making at least 28 knots.

All this was taking place at 12:15 P.M. at the narrowest part of the Channel, within easy reach of the English coast. Was the British lion asleep—or did he take this for a phantasmal apparition, a mirage, something that simply could not be true? These Germans might be given credit for a good deal but clearly nobody over there could believe their tiny fleet was making a getaway through the Channel in broad daylight, under the very noses of the British shore batteries with their radar, past dozens of airfields and the ports where M.T.B.'s and torpedo boats were lying in wait, right through the mine fields threatening the path of any German ships that tried to slink through along the Continental coast. . . .

The men on Cape Gris-Nez waved their caps as they watched a naval review the like of which had never been seen before. Then the squadron swung round the promontory, setting its course northeast, with the narrowest part of the Channel behind it—and still not a finger had been raised to stop it.

Only a month earlier not more than a handful of men had known that so daring an operation was being planned. On January 12, 1942, a special train of only two carriages was rolling from Berlin to Rastenburg in East Prussia. In the compartment reserved for conferences Grossadmiral Raeder was explaining the plan to a few high naval officers whom he had suddenly summoned to Berlin the day before:

"Gentlemen, we all are convinced we cannot leave the ships in Brest any longer. For the past eight months the enemy has dropped his bombs wide of the target over and over again, but I feel this cannot be much longer the case. Only the other day the three hundredth aerial attack on the dockyards at Brest was carried out. . . ."

The few opportunities for training available to the crew, their absolute lack of battle experience, and the general position in the Atlantic made any undertaking on the old pattern out of the question. Besides, there was always the duty reconnaissance aircraft permanently over the harbor entrance, ready to inform the British Admiralty of the slightest movement on the part of the German ships.

"If we were to take the ships by the northern route round Scotland, the entire journey would fall within the province of the enemy air force and they would be bound to fall in with the superior British battle fleet—in itself a very great risk. The only other possibility is to make a dash through the Channel. I am aware, of course, that in this case too the risk is no less great, and that the undertaking will only be feasible if the enemy is so taken by surprise that he has no time to take effective counter-measures."

For hours the pros and cons of the situation were debated. A break-through of this kind within sight of the enemy coast was without precedent, would be in utter defiance of all tradition as regards the use of capital ships. Eventually the Chief of Naval Staff closed the conference with the words:

"Remember that the Führer himself will make the final decision. So when you give him your opinion, do not minimize the dangers, but don't be too pessimistic either. That's the only way we can contribute toward saving the ships."

At four in the afternoon the admirals were facing Hitler in his "Wolf's Lair" near Rastenburg. Since December, 1941, he had been haunted by the fear that the Allies would land in Norway to threaten his northern flank, and it was for this reason that he proposed bringing the three battleships of the High Seas Fleet from Brest to the north.

Now once again every possibility was passed under review, with this time Jeschonnek and Galland of the Luftwaffe also present. In the face of general agreement that the chances were only fifty-fifty, Hitler nevertheless finally decided that the break-through was the only way out.

"If the ships remain in Brest," he said, "there is no doubt that they will eventually be put out of action by the enemy air force. It's like the case of a man with cancer. If I don't operate, he must die, slowly but surely. If I operate, he *may* be saved. Therefore let us operate!"

In this way the venture was started which was later to be acknowledged by friend and foe alike as an outstanding daring combined operation of the German Navy and Luftwaffe. Its success was entirely dependent on the maintenance of secrecy, the carrying out of all the preparations necessary without the British smelling a rat. Among other things, there was the terribly difficult job of camouflaging the concentration of whole flotillas of mine sweepers, which were to clear a road free of mines, the so-called *Prachtstrasse* or royal road from Brest along the whole extent of the French, Belgian, and Dutch coasts as far as the Bay of Helgoland.

The fictitious reasons for this maneuver invented by the few officers who were in the secret were amazing. The *Prachtstrasse* had to be ready in a matter of four weeks' time. Its entire length was accordingly divided up into hundreds of sections, and a plausible, natural reason for clearing the mines in each section was provided. Spurious agency reports were circulated according to which new enemy mine fields had been laid, whose presence had to be investigated. Vessels supposedly about to break the blockade were produced for which a road had to be cleared. It was also given out that we were about to lay mine fields of our own, which necessitated finding out whether the area in question had already been covered by the enemy. . . .

So it went on day after day, section by section. The mine sweepers had frequently to change their course, zigzagging around in the most erratic way, so that their commanders often shook their heads and began to doubt the sanity of the Admiral in Paris. They had not the foggiest notion of what they were preparing—how could they have guessed that the sum total of their deviations, marked in a top-secret chart in Paris, marked the mine-free Channel?

At the end of January three young officers who had been navigating in the Channel since 1940 and knew it like their own pocket were summoned to Paris. Here for ten days they found themselves locked in a room with a sentry at the door. As they had committed no crime, they were given everything they wanted, except their personal liberty; their task was the complicated one of studying the charts on which the mine-free area was marked. These officers, who were to act as the warships' pilots, were not "released" until after the end of the operation.

When they arrived at Brest in a closed black limousine . . .

"What do you say you are?" the *Gneisenau's* commander asked them suspiciously. "Mine-sweeping officers? What are you doing on board my ship, then?"

Was it possible that even the ships' commanders had not been initiated into the secret?

Two more days. The timing of the operation could not be altered, depending as it did on the tides—the one thing one couldn't do anything about. Meanwhile army trucks loaded with khaki uniforms drew up on the pier. Then the Navy ordered several thousand sun helmets—with a request to keep the order secret. There was no reason to doubt that the agencies would be informed about it in a couple of hours.

The fact that the ships were preparing to put to sea could not be concealed. So when the story of the tropical kit got out Brest was buzzing with rumors.

"We're in for a good time, boys—off to the sunny South!"

"A cruise in the South Atlantic. . . ."

"We're going to capture the Azores. . . ."

The High Command was not at all displeased with these rumors, as not a soul had found out what was really being planned.

Sailing time was scheduled for 8:00 P.M. on February 11, 1942. The crews were made to carry out a battle exercise to camouflage the fact that the ships were raising steam.

At a few minutes before eight the sirens howled—enemy aircraft approaching! It would be the limit if anything were to happen now! All went well, however, but two hours were lost, two hours which though they delayed the start yet possibly saved the entire operation.

At that precise moment the radar of the duty reconnaissance aircraft on duty went out of action, and he did not notice that the German squadron had sailed. By the time he was relieved, the ships had already passed through the critical area.

During the aircraft alarm General Koller of the Luftwaffe had hit on an excellent idea. He at once made his way through the dense artificial fog which enveloped the whole of the harbor to Admiral Ciliax, in command of the break-through, who was waiting impatiently on board the *Scharnhorst*.

"Can you go to sea in this fog?" he asked.

Ciliax pondered a moment.

"Yes, it could be done, but the enemy aircraft . . . ."

"Splendid! Listen: I'll let you know as soon as the British aircraft have gone, and then you leave harbor. But we'll leave the aircraft warning on till tomorrow morning, and the artificial fog as well. Then the spies won't notice you are going out to sea."

That was exactly what did happen. By the time a British patrol boat sighted the squadron, it was eleven o'clock the next morning, the most dangerous mine fields had been by-passed, and the ships were steaming at full speed for the narrowest part of the Channel.

At first nobody in London took the report seriously. It was known the Germans were planning something, and precautions had been taken by laying more mines along the Continental coast, but on the morning of February 12 nobody was bothering about the German battleships. London had something else to worry about: since the night before every radar set on the English coast had ceased to function! For the first time the Germans were operating their jamming stations in a big way. From a wavelength of 11 meters down to 80 centimeters not a single British radar instrument was able to function. This had put the whole air-attack-warning system out of action—England was expecting a full-dress raid by the Luftwaffe at any moment. The feint had succeeded. Meanwhile the German squadron was calmly continuing on its way, undiscovered. When it was sighted at last, the British Admiralty refused to believe it.

"The Germans? If they come, it'll be at dead of night, not at noon!"

At 1:15 P.M. the squadron's distance from Dover was increasing, but gradually the Germans began to have misgivings. There was something queer about it—surely the English must have sighted the ships long ago!

At that precise moment the big guns on the island flashed out for the first time. It was high time, too, for in a quarter of an hour the squadron would be out of range of the coastal batteries. It had been steaming along for an hour and a half before the first shot was fired. Now the outside E boats were firing smoke shells, and the gunfire from the shore had ceased. If only it all went as well as that!

When the British defenses had recovered from their initial surprise and sounded the alarm, the German ships had already reached the Belgian coast. The first to attack were six naval torpedo bombers, led by the Captain Esmonde who had secured the decisive hits on the *Bismarck* ten months earlier. All six were shot down by German Focke-Wulf and Messerschmitt fighters.

The next on the scene were M.T.B.'s followed by—bombers —destroyers—and more bombers. Hell broke loose, all the German ships opening fire with all they had. The *Gneisenau* and the *Prinz Eugen* succeeded several times in avoiding the track of a torpedo by skillful maneuvering. In three hours the British lost a considerable number of aircraft. Unremittingly the ships continued on their course and soon reached the Dutch coast.

At 3:28 P.M. the hull of the *Scharnhorst*, which was leading, received a heavy blow from below which seemed to lift her bodily out of the water. Right up to the commander's bridge, everything was flung about. Many of the crew were literally lifted off their feet and then smacked violently down. The ship had run on a mine.

A few seconds later reports came in from all sections: *Electric installations failed. No light on the ship. Rudder does not function. Gyro-compass out of action. Turret Anton taking water. Fires in all boilers extinguished.*

Admiral Ciliax was looking worried. Too bad this should happen just now. . . . The reports did not sound encouraging, either; there seemed little hope of repairing the ship quickly. However, the commander had to continue leading the squadron. Destroyer 38 was informed by signals: *Stand by to take Admiral on board.* The transfer was a risky business. As Destroyer 38 vanished in the haze, steaming at full speed in the wake of the disappearing squadron, the *Scharnhorst* dropped astern alone, protected by only a few units, rolling in the deserted waters.

However, everybody on board got feverishly to work, the technical personnel surpassing itself. If only the British refrained from making another concentrated attack, it might be possible to get the ship going once more. After 12 minutes the Chief Engineer reported the boilers had just been lit again. The ship had taken in "only" 200 tons of water. The first good reports were already coming in:

Main armament has electric current again. E-machine running.

Thank God, now they were able to fire again! At 3:49 P.M., 20 minutes after the *Scharnhorst* had struck the mine, the port engine was working once more.

Emergency full speed ahead!

After half an hour the ship was chasing the others at top speed. Suddenly a destroyer appeared right ahead—Destroyer 38, lying there with her engines stopped.

"Excuse me, sir," the navigating officer said to his commander on the bridge of the *Scharnhorst,* "I think we shall have to reduce speed, else the Admiral will get wet."

When later back at home Admiral Ciliax went on board the *Scharnhorst* his mien was radiant: "Boys, when I saw you looming out of the mist with your white mustache in front, I could have shouted with joy."

In London, and in the entire British press, a storm of indignation arose. How could this have happened under their very eyes? On February 14, 1942, the *Times* wrote:

"Vice-Admiral Ciliax has succeeded where the Duke of Medina Sidonia failed. . . . Nothing more mortifying to the pride of sea power has happened in home waters since the seventeenth century."

5

The *Graf Spee*

After the successful break-through up the English Channel Admiral Raeder again had a small but powerful striking force available with which to resume the offensive. This was also a great weight off Hitler's mind. As usual he had been kept informed of every detail of the Channel break-through at his *Wolfsschanze* headquarters.

To him, a landlubber who had no comprehension of the sea or of naval warfare, our great battleships from the moment he came in contact with them were something unimaginably awe-inspiring. When as Reichs Chancellor in 1934 he had his first experience of firing practice in the Baltic on board the *Deutschland* his profound emotion at the spectacle was clearly written on his face, and the deep impression of this first contact with the vague potentialities of sea power never left him.

In the years that followed, no German capital ship was launched without Hitler's being present if he could manage it. In his imagination, in which imposing objects played a very important part, battleships were to become symbols of the might of Germany. These powerful monsters made such an impression on his mind that he just could not conceive that one of them could be lost or sunk in battle. The very first months of the war had brought a tremendous disillusionment: the loss of the *Admiral Graf Spee,* the most modern of the three armored ships which Germany had been allowed to build by the Treaty of Versailles.

This loss brought the curtain down on the drama enacted between the thirteenth and the seventeenth of December, 1939, far from Germany and a Europe at war, in the broad estuary of the River Plate off the coast of neutral Uruguay. Shortly after 6:00 P.M. on December 17 the *Graf Spee* weighed anchor under the eyes of a crowd of many thousands gathered in the harbor of Montevideo. Two hours before the expiration of the time allowed her to stay there by the Uruguayan authorities she steamed slowly out through the narrow channel toward the open sea. But there the British warships were standing watch—about whose strength and numbers the wildest rumors had been current in Montevideo for days—in order to give the *coup de grâce* with united forces to the adversary for whom they had vainly waited for so long.

The many thousands on shore who were hoping for the unique chance of witnessing the apparently inevitable battle had their reward, but in quite a different way to what they had expected. The German freighter *Tacoma* which had sought shelter in the neutral harbor of Montevideo at the outbreak of the war followed in the wake of the battleship. Was she now trying to run for it under the protection of the latter's guns, attempting a break-through for home while the other faced a battle for life and death?

Such uncertainties heightened the excitement of the watching crowd. Through their field glasses many of them could make out something curious happening: the German ships were stopping at about the three-mile limit. Suddenly there had appeared on the scene two seagoing tugs and a lighter which must have come across from Buenos Aires. These and other still smaller craft moved back and forth between the battleship and the freighter. Details could no longer be made out from the shore; the distance was now too great. What did it mean? What was going on out there?

At last, at five minutes to eight, a terrific jet of flame suddenly burst from the deck of the *Graf Spee;* in an instant a black cloud formed and rose high into the sky, and a second later an explosion like a distant growl of thunder smote the ears of the listening thousands. No doubt was possible: the *Graf Spee* had been blown up; the Germans had scuttled their own ship!

The news of the sensational end of the "phantom ship" spread like wildfire across the globe. Everywhere guesses were made and arguments debated—as they still are today—as to how she came to this end. Why did her commanding officer, Captain Langsdorff, make this certainly very hard decision to scuttle his ship without fighting it out with the enemy? How was he brought to bay at the mouth of the River Plate?

On Monday, August 21, 1939, the *Admiral Graf Spee* left Wilhelmshaven steaming northward. This was nothing exceptional, nor was there anything unusual to be remarked on board. Perhaps she was going out on a training cruise or for battle practice, involving either a stay at sea for several days or a call in at another port—nobody knew or thought any more about it.

A few days later, however, the ship had become more interesting—she had disappeared. She had not returned to harbor and no one could say what had become of her. At the same time, too, the British Admiralty got wind of this mysterious affair. "One or two armored ships," it was announced, "have left their home bases and it has so far been impossible to discover their whereabouts."

Were the Germans trying to bring their "pocket battleships" unobserved out of the "wet triangle" of the North Sea to move them to favorable positions with a view to attacking and sinking British shipping immediately on an outbreak of war between Great Britain and Germany? These were questions on which the British Admiralty had to have certainty. A number of ships of the Home Fleet were dispatched to the sea lanes lying between Greenland, Iceland, the Shetlands, and the Orkneys, with instructions to keep their eyes peeled. Yet their vigilance was in vain; not one of them was able to report having sighted a foreign warship. That was not surprising, for at that time the *Graf Spee* and the *Deutschland,* which was also at large, had already passed beyond the above-named channels and had vanished into the Atlantic.

Even after the declaration of war nothing was heard of them for weeks. At last, on September 30, two lifeboats drifted ashore near Pernambuco on the northeast promontory of Brazil. Excitedly the occupants reported that their ship, the 500-ton British cargo vessel *Clement,* had been stopped by a large German battleship and sunk.

Grave confirmation as this news was of the fears entertained in London, there was none the less relief at the Admiralty that they were now no longer groping in the dark. A German raider was menacing the safety of the South Atlantic; that much was established and countermeasures could therefore be put in hand. A little while later another British ship was sunk, but this time on the North Atlantic route. Was it possible that the "phantom ship," as it was now called, could have traveled those many thousand miles in so short an interval to leave another "visiting card" so far up north? It seemed hardly credible. However, the news that came in almost immediately afterward that the three freighters, the *Ashley* (4229 tons), the *Newton Beach* (4661 tons), and the *Huntsman* (8300 tons) had vanished off the west coast of Africa removed all doubt. A single raider could not be simultaneously on the prowl off South America, in the North Atlantic, and in West African waters. There must therefore be more than one raider.

After these reports the British Admiralty had no option but to form a number of special squadrons to hunt down these German commerce raiders. Their mission was not so easy. In the first place, to locate a lone enemy, always prepared to run for it, in the illimitable vastness of the oceans was a task that needed a handsome measure of luck, and, secondly, each of these squadrons had to be, at least theoretically, superior to the German ship. With a speed of 28 knots these pocket battleships were, however, faster than their more heavily armed pursuers and with their six 11-inch guns more powerful than the Allies' smaller but faster vessels.

Nine such squadrons were formed with difficulty by the Naval Staff. Not less than 23 capital ships—four battleships, 14 cruisers, and five aircraft carriers—were withdrawn from other duties because they were needed for the phantom chase. It put the British to a vast amount of trouble, and that was exactly the intention of the German Naval High Command.

In its directives to the captains of the *Graf Spee* and the *Deutschland* the latter had issued the following orders:

1. Your mission is to reach the Atlantic unobserved, and even there you are at first to avoid every ship that appears on the horizon. These instructions must be obeyed even after hostilities may have broken out between Great Britain and Germany until you receive a radio order to go into action.

2. Your mission is then to disrupt and strangle enemy shipping by every available means. You are as far as possible to avoid contact with enemy naval forces. Even inferior warships should only be engaged if such action is conducive to your main task of interference with the enemy's supply lines.

3. Frequent change of location in the operational area will have the effect of bewildering the enemy and will at the same time obstruct shipping, even if no directly perceptible results are achieved. Evasive action from time to time in remote sea areas will likewise increase the enemy's perplexity.

These were the orders which governed the activity of the German phantom ships. Sir Winston Churchill writes in his memoirs:

"With all this wisdom the British Admiralty would have been in rueful agreement."

In November the *Graf Spee* left another visiting card, this time in the Indian Ocean, by sinking a small tanker off the coast of East Africa. Doubtless she could have found more important prey on the busy shipping routes that converge at Aden, but she was less concerned with piling up a high score of sinkings than with creating a general nervousness and misleading her pursuers. With this in view she immediately doubled back circuitously around the Cape of Good Hope into the South Atlantic. There, in the space of a few days, on the much-frequented route from Cape Town to Freetown three ships were again sent to the bottom. But there also the luck which had been with the German raider began to turn.

One of these three freighters, namely the *Doric Star*, which was bagged on December 2, had on board an intrepid radio operator. He paid not the slightest attention to the *Graf Spee's* order that the radio must not be touched, nor did he let himself be intimidated by the warning shots fired by the battleship, but blithely continued to send out a nonstop SOS, repeatedly giving the exact position of the encounter with the raider.

On the bridge of his ship Captain Langsdorff angrily lowered the binoculars through which he had been observing the *Doric Star*.

"That's a hell of a fellow," he growled. "His damned signals will bring the whole British fleet about our ears."

His irritation was understandable, for now the excursion into the Indian Ocean which he had undertaken with the object of deceiving the enemy must be all to no purpose. Langsdorff could picture the relief with which the commanders of the Allied naval squadrons doubtless searching for him at that moment would receive the *Doric Star's* precise report of just where the *Graf Spee* was lurking.

Still, that did not mean that they had caught him, not by a long sight. Undesirable as the new situation was for the German ship, her captain was determined to make the best of it. The disclosure of his momentary location might also be turned to good account, for while the enemy would certainly concentrate their search in the area where he was known to be, he could leave his field of operations before they arrived on the scene and disappear again on the other side of the Atlantic.

"We shall remain here for another day or two," he informed his officers. "I don't think the British forces are near enough to pick us up before that. Then we will make ourselves scarce for a few days in unfrequented waters."

"We fixed our next meeting with the *Altmark* for December 4, sir," one of his officers reminded him.

"That fits in admirably," laughed Langsdorff. "I daresay we shall make a good haul around here tomorrow, and then we can push off for our rendezvous."

The modern tanker and cargo ship *Altmark* was at the beck and call of the *Graf Spee*, whose raiding expedition would not have been possible without her, for unlike the Allies the Germans had no bases outside Europe where they could refuel and take in stores. When the two ships met on December 4 at the prearranged rendezvous Captain Langsdorff's prognostication had already been fulfilled: a large, modern refrigerator ship had fallen into his toils and been sunk, bringing his total of sinkings from September 30 to almost 50,000 tons. Thus, having caused a great deal of confusion into the bargain, the *Graf Spee* could be well satisfied with her achievement. Nevertheless, she had been at sea uninterruptedly from August 21, her engines had been running day after day, night after night, and it was high time to think of turning for home in order to give the ship a thorough refit.

Langsdorff had also been right in his surmise about the effect of the *Doric Star's* radio signals. He had already made off before the British naval forces arrived on the scene of his activities. These comprised two of the nine squadrons and if he had lingered much longer he might well have been in trouble. They were Force H, with the heavy cruisers *Sussex* and *Shropshire*, and Force K with the battle cruiser *Renown* and the aircraft carrier *Ark Royal*. But by then the Germans had already vanished again.

The captain of the German raider, however, was deceiving himself if he believed that all the British ships on the lookout for him in the South Atlantic would without exception hasten to the West African coast on reception of the *Doric Star's* message, leaving other profitable shipping routes unprotected. There was, first of all, Commodore Harwood, in command of Force G, who had no intention whatever of removing his four cruisers, *Cumberland, Exeter, Ajax,* and *Achilles,* from their stations off the River Plate.

"Sooner or later," argued the Commodore, "the phantom ship is bound to turn up here too. We have only to have the patience to wait for her."

And this exactly hit the nail on the head. For the traffic from the River Plate to England was a very enticing objective. And when could the *Graf Spee* find a more favorable moment to send to the bottom a few fully laden ships than now when it was assumed that the British were still off the west coast of Africa?

At all events Captain Langsdorff decided to pay a brief visit to South America before finally heading for home—a decision which was to prove the undoing of his ship and of himself.

As day dawned on December 13, 1939, the *Graf Spee* was steaming at normal cruising speed on a southeasterly course away from the coast of Brazil, having ventured the previous day to within about a 150 miles of it. In this way the raider was bound to cross the shipping routes from the north and the northeast to the River Plate, Buenos Aires, and Montevideo. Here there was every prospect of rich booty. And indeed the sun had barely been up for half an hour when the lookout suddenly reported from the foretop, the highest point of the ship:

"Masts in sight right ahead."

Exactly in the direction in which the battleship was steaming faint lines had appeared above the horizon. They must be ship's masts, and this in itself was suspicious, for if it were a cargo steamer in all probability the first thing to be seen would have been the smoke from her funnel. But masts without smoke indicated a warship.

The captain was roused. Only he could decide what was to be done. There was still plenty of time to turn away, and it was preferable to disappear again rather than run the risk of a disagreeable surprise. For obviously the *Graf Spee* had not yet been spotted by the ships on the distant horizon. Yes, there was more than one ship, as could now be made out distinctly from the foretop. And the position of the masts made it pretty certain that they were on a northeasterly course, that is, traveling on an opposite course to the *Graf Spee*. Any alteration, of course, especially one made toward the German ship, would be seen by the lookouts at the masthead and instantly reported to the bridge. But for the moment nothing of the sort happened.

As, however, the *Graf Spee* maintained her course, the adversaries rapidly drew nearer to each other. Langsdorff could not and would not make the decision to run from a danger which was still hypothetical only.

Meanwhile the superstructure of the enemy ships had appeared above the horizon and at first it was reckoned that they must be a cruiser and two destroyers. In any case the German was more than a match for such opponents. But did not the High Command's operational orders lay down that any engagement even with weaker naval forces was, if possible, to be avoided? There was still ample time to put about, although meanwhile the German ship must surely have also been discovered by the enemy. In spite of this Captain Langsdorff gave the order:

"Clear the decks for action."

He was still puzzled. What was a cruiser doing here with two destroyers? It looked very much like a convoy escort. Perhaps the escort had gone on ahead and the merchant ships would presently also appear on the horizon.

Consider: a convoy! Would it not crown the success of the raider's foray if the *Graf Spee* could at one blow increase her score by several ships? Langsdorff was confident of being able to deal with the escort without himself suffering any appreciable damage. The High Command's orders had expressly left him a loophole for this contingency: he was free to engage the enemy if such action were necessary to further the main objective—the destruction of the enemy's supplies.

To be sure, there was not as yet any sign of a convoy. Instead, it was soon evident that the cruiser was a heavy cruiser of

10,000 tons with an armament inferior to the *Graf Spee's* only in the caliber of her heavy guns, for she had six 8-inch guns to the German's six 11-inch guns. And the two other ships which had at first been mistaken for destroyers now turned out to be light cruisers with sixteen 6-inch guns between them.

When this new situation was established beyond any shadow of doubt, Captain Langsdorff looked from one to another of his officers on the bridge, lit a fresh cigar, and merely remarked:

"Well, what are we waiting for?"

Then he went up into the foretop to command his ship from there during the engagement.

In the meantime Commodore Harwood—for it was he with three of his cruisers, *Exeter, Ajax,* and *Achilles*—divided his forces so as to attack the raider from several sides and so disperse the concentrated firepower of the *Graf Spee's* heavy guns.

But Langsdorff had evidently no intention of playing the enemy's game. His plan was to finish off his adversaries one by one and to concentrate his fire first on the strongest and most formidable, the heavy cruiser *Exeter*. At 6:16 A.M. on December 13, 1939, the first broadside of the 11-inch triple turrets launched its thunder against the enemy. Three minutes later the *Exeter* replied. Meanwhile the range had visibly decreased and the ships were little more than 15 miles apart. Both ships maintained a very high rate of fire and the Germans could soon observe the first direct hits on the *Exeter,* fires and wreaths of black smoke being the first perceptible results.

But some of the British shells had also found their mark. The first hit completely wrecked the galley; later the damage proved to be serious when it was found that the drinking-water supply had ceased to function. Other shells hit the torpedo room, the flak-control position, and various living quarters. There were a number of casualties. Splinters whizzed up even into the foretop and the captain at his lofty post sustained a superficial wound.

But all this was as nothing to the hell which had broken loose on board the *Exeter*. In barely an hour she received over a hundred serious hits; she began to heel over and was soon no more than a mass of smoke and flame which might be expected to blow up at any moment. Five of her six heavy guns had been put out of action, but still the last remaining gun continued to fire unflinchingly.

When Commodore Harwood, who had described a wide circle with the *Ajax* and the *Achilles,* saw the plight of the *Exeter,* he closed at high speed to engage the enemy and relieve the crippled ship. He was completely successful; the very first broadside from his 6-inch guns registered a direct hit on the *Graf Spee,* knocking out a 6-inch gun and killing the entire crew. For better or for worse, much as he would have liked to finish off the *Exeter,* Langsdorff had to turn his attention to his new assailant.

And now he had to pay for his carelessness in letting the two light cruisers get so close. Regardless of the superiority of the battleship, they fearlessly attacked and deluged her with a veritable hail of shells. It was, of course, almost out of the question that they could score any decisive hits with their 6-inch guns. Yet every shell that tore into the steel hull of the *Graf Spee* brought damage or casualties.

Langsdorff now staked everything on one card. If he had succeeded in putting the heavy cruiser out of action he must surely be able to deal with the two light cruisers. So he now turned his full, unimpaired fire power upon the *Ajax* and the *Achilles,* which were by now at a range of only four to five miles. But fortune favored them; they received only a few serious hits. By means of sharp alterations, of course, and by the use of funnel and artificial smoke, they understood perfectly how to avoid the deadly salvos of 11-inch shells. The German gunnery officer was in despair.

"I think our base-fused heavy shells must be passing clean through the lightly built cruisers and only exploding when they strike the water and can do no harm."

"We will try opening the range," replied the captain through the control telephone; "then our 11-inch guns will be more effective and their 6-inch guns no use."

At full speed ahead the battleship tried to draw out of range of the enemy's guns. But Commodore Harwood had no difficulty in holding on to her. His cruisers were in fact faster and their engines so far undamaged.

"We must hit them," Langsdorff barked to his gunners, "at least badly enough to make them reduce speed. Otherwise we shall have the two cruisers on our tails for good, shadowing us until the heavy forces can come up."

"We must hit them," said Harwood likewise, "or else they'll escape us yet."

At this moment two direct hits crashed into the *Ajax*, smashing both the after turrets. Four 6-inch guns were silenced at one blow. Commodore Harwood realized that things were getting serious.

The damaging effect of the hits had also been observed on board the *Graf Spee*, where it aroused fresh hope. Suddenly the tracks of several torpedoes drove their way toward the battleship—but as they were spotted in time it was possible to take avoiding action. And then what Langsdorff had been praying for happened at last: the British cruisers were turning away and dropping steadily astern. For a while they remained within effective range of the 11-inch guns; then they passed out of range. Had they finally had enough? Had their engines succumbed at last?

No, it was only that after the serious hits on the *Ajax* Commodore Harwood had changed his tactics. Hardly was he out of range of the German heavy artillery, to which he had prudently decided not to expose himself any further, than he proceeded to cling to the heels of the phantom ship with no intention of ever letting her out of his sight again.

Captain Langsdorff, however, hoped to be able to shake off his shadowers. Now that the guns were silent he immediately made a first round of inspection of the ship and convinced himself of the damage she had sustained. Although the engines and the heavy guns were still intact, she had received several very unpleasant hits, including, worst of all, a yawning hole in her side which it would be impossible to repair with her own resources at sea. For the moment it was not particularly serious, but in a gale or heavy seaway it might well endanger the ship. And what a long voyage lay ahead before the *Graf Spee* could be in harbor back at home! A voyage on which they would be especially dependent on their sea-keeping qualities, for the incessant fighting had seriously depleted the stores of ammunition and they could not permit themselves the luxury of another encounter such as this.

When Langsdorff finally made the decision to put in to a neutral port and there to rush through the most urgently needed repairs he was probably swayed by consideration for the severely wounded on board. There were nearly 30 of these—besides 36 dead—whom he was anxious should be transferred to medical care and attention on shore. He believed that it would not be long before he could put to sea again, at any rate before the enemy had time to bring up superior forces, and that he could then take the risk of breaking through for home in better condition than he was at the moment.

And so the armored ship *Admiral Graf Spee* entered "the trap of Montevideo"—the expression used by the captain a few days later. Langsdorff would have preferred to put in to Buenos Aires because the Argentine government was more friendly to the Germans than the Uruguayan. His only reason for deciding on Montevideo was that it would be quicker to put to sea again from there, whereas the Argentine capital lay too far upstream.

And now the world had its sensation: There had been a battle at sea! The German raider had taken refuge in a neutral port! It was true that even with a good pair of binoculars no damage could be detected, but the damage must be there, otherwise why had the *Graf Spee* abandoned her strongest weapon, invisibility?

No illusions were harbored at the British Admiralty. The

Ajax and the *Achilles*, battered as they had been, would not be able to stop the *Graf Spee* if she put to sea again in two or at most three days. The heavy cruiser *Cumberland* was a more hopeful proposition. She was steaming north at all speed from the Falkland Islands to take the place of the crippled *Exeter*. To be sure, the *Cumberland* could not be off the mouth of the River Plate before December 17, three days hence. The aircraft carrier *Ark Royal* and the battle cruiser *Renown*—at last a force superior to the German ship—were up in the north off Pernambuco and would have to cover a good 2500 miles to reach the River Plate. As, moreover, these ships would have to refuel at Rio de Janeiro, their intervention could hardly be reckoned with before the end of a week.

But wait: how would it be if it were put out that these powerful units had already arrived off Montevideo?

The battle which now began was not fought with guns. It was a cold war, a war of nerves, of inspired reports and threats, of rumors and speculations. At this particular moment Captain Langsdorff was more susceptible to this insidious poison than he would otherwise have been. What weighty decisions he had to make! The Uruguayan government was careful to give him no support. With difficulty he obtained permission for his ship to stay in harbor for 72 hours. The repair was purposely delayed. Little progress was made, and meantime the hours were running out, the precious hours that spelled life and freedom. Also, his wound must have left its mark upon the man who was now faced with so many vital decisions.

The senior officers of the German Naval High Command heard with grave faces the conclusions Langsdorff had drawn from the situation. It was December 16. Grossadmiral Raeder had summoned a meeting of the "small circle" of his most intimate colleagues.

"Gentlemen, Langsdorff has made us a signal," the C.-in-C. began. "He sees the strategic situation off Montevideo as follows: *In addition to cruisers and destroyers, Ark Royal and Renown.*

Close blockade at night. A break-out into the open sea and a break-through for home hopeless. What do you say to that?"

Fregattenkapitän Wagner, the real brains of the operations branch, replied: "This enemy situation is new to me. According to our information, which is admittedly not 100 per cent certain, it is impossible for the *Ark Royal* and the *Renown* to be off the River Plate."

"But we may be wide of the mark," interposed the Chief of Staff, Admiral Schniewind. "We are basing our judgment on such reports and information as have reached us. We cannot tell whether this information is always correct. But Langsdorff is on the spot. If he reports the presence of heavy enemy units he must have made certain of his facts."

There was no possible answer to this. Captain Langsdorff was one of the ablest officers in the German Navy. The Grossadmiral had implicit confidence in him and even had the intention of later promoting him to the post of Chief of the Operations Division of the Naval Staff in the narrow circle of the very few men who decided the conduct of the war at sea.

"Let me read you the rest of Langsdorff's report: *Propose taking out ship as far as limit of neutral waters. If possible to fight way through to Buenos Aires will attempt it. In case break-through involves certain destruction of Graf Spee without chance of inflicting damage on enemy request decision whether ship should be scuttled in mouth of River Plate in spite of in-sufficient depth of water or whether internment preferred. Captain Graf Spee.* It is, of course, open to question, gentlemen, whether an internment at Montevideo would not in the end amount to the same thing as capture undamaged by the enemy."

"Naturally, Uruguay's neutrality cannot be trusted. She is far too weak to withstand strong pressure by France and Great Britain."

"Very well then, internment at Montevideo is not to be considered," Raeder concluded, summing up the general opinion. "We must inform Langsdorff to that effect. But otherwise we ought to leave him a free hand."

This was the old principle which Raeder had held ever since the Battle of Jutland in the First World War and which he believed the only right one: a captain must be master on his own bridge. The captain knew the situation best, and he must make the decision, not the staff officers around the conference table far away at home.

But would it not have been possible, without worrying him with orders, to have made the captain's decisions easier by giving him some advice? Could he not have been told that doubts existed as to the correctness of his appreciation of the enemy situation; above all, that according to the information available to the Naval Staff the British heavy ships could hardly be off Montevideo?

On the other hand, Langsdorff enjoyed the complete confidence of the High Command. It was taken for granted that his decisions would be made to the best of his knowledge of the existing situation, and the Grossadmiral backed him up to the hilt. Even Hitler, whom Raeder promptly informed of the situation, raised no objections. (In particular, he had never been in direct telephonic communication with Langsdorff nor did he order his suicide, as was afterward suggested by the Americans.)

Thus Raeder's signaled reply left the captain of the *Graf Spee* complete freedom of action with the sole proviso that he must not allow himself to be interned in Uruguay. The last sentence read:

If the ship is scuttled do your best to make her destruction complete. Raeder.

The following day, December 17, 1939, at five minutes to eight in the evening the armored ship *Admiral Graf Spee* was blown up. The towering cloud of black smoke, the fires that raged for days in the wreck still projecting above the surface of the water, the gaping hull, and the steel plates hurtled through the air testified to the force of the explosion. The ship was indeed permanently destroyed. The few members of the crew who remained on board until the last moment had exploded torpedo warheads in the ammunition magazines. . . .

The captain had cleverly paved the way for the transfer of the crew to the Argentine, where they were interned. On December 19 he addressed his men for the last time to inspire them with courage and confidence for the time ahead of them. He ended with these words:

"It will surely be debated all over the world whether the destruction of our ship was right or not, whether it would not have been braver to have resumed the battle with the enemy and to have died a sailor's death. Each one of us would have done that gladly, without a murmur. I propose giving you proof that I myself was not lacking in personal courage."

The men did not gather the implication of these words until the following morning. Captain Langsdorff was found dead in his room, where he had shot himself.

In his last letter, which he addressed to the German ambassador in Buenos Aires, he wrote:

"Your Excellency, after a long struggle I have decided to destroy the battleship *Admiral Graf Spee* in order to prevent her falling into enemy hands. I am firmly convinced that this was the only possible decision once my ship had been led into the trap of Montevideo. For with the ammunition remaining any attempt to fight or to reach the open sea was foredoomed to failure. And I could only have sunk the ship in deep water after having used up all my ammunition. Instead of exposing my ship to the risk of falling wholly or partially into the hands of the enemy after a gallant fight, I have decided not to fight, but to use the ammunition to destroy all installations and to sink the ship. . . . I have made up my mind to stand the consequences of this decision, for a captain with a sense of honor does not need to be told that his fate is indissolubly linked with his ship's fate. I shall have no further chance of taking an active part in my country's present struggle. I can only prove by my death that the members of the armed forces of the Third Reich are ready to die for the honor of the flag. I alone bear the responsibility for the destruction of the battleship *Admiral Graf Spee*. I am happy to be able to give my life to efface any conceivable blot upon the honor of the flag, and I shall meet my fate in a firm belief in the justice of our cause and in the future of my people and my Führer.

"Your Excellency, I write you this letter in the calm of evening after due deliberation in order to place you in a position to inform my superiors and to be able to counter rumors should this be necessary.

"Langsdorff, Captain, commanding the
battleship *Admiral Graf Spee*"

6

No Unnecessary Risks!

THE PICTURES OF THE BLAZING, SHATTERED WRECK OF the *Graf Spee* which were reproduced the world over made an indelible impression on Hitler, who now for the first time perceived the chasm opening up between the world of his fantasies and reality.

The satisfaction it had given him when just previously the *Deutschland* had been renamed *Lützow* for political reasons was characteristic. That a ship named *Deutschland* might possibly be sunk was a doubly intolerable thought. And similarly in later years he was always to be in a state of extreme irritability and nervous tension whenever any operation involving big ships was being carried out. When the *Admiral Scheer* was cruising in the Indian Ocean at the beginning of 1941, Hitler would rush up to every high naval officer who approached him with the question: "How is the *Scheer* doing?"

This nervousness was also responsible for Hitler's attitude during the confusing events of New Year's Eve and New Year's Day, 1943, which were to lead to one of the gravest crises that ever faced the German Navy.

During the night of December 31, 1942, Admiral Kummetz was shivering on the bridge of his flagship, the heavy cruiser *Admiral Hipper,* as she steamed in a heavy swell toward the northwest, 26 miles from the Norwegian coast. It was bitterly cold, and from time to time a shower of hail struck the decks. Visibility was nil; even the three escorting destroyers could not be seen, to say nothing of the second heavy ship of the squadron, the *Lützow,* which, accompanied by three more destroyers, was lying on the same course some 20 miles to the south.

All the same, nothing could go wrong now, the Admiral thought. Somewhere to the northwest the German cruisers and destroyers must light upon a convoy stuffed to the brim with war material for Russia—if their calculations were correct. U boats were shadowing the convoy and transmitting homing signals at hourly intervals. Accordingly, they must come to grips with the adversary the next morning, provided he did not double on his tracks. The radio intelligence service had also discovered that the British had left their battleships at home— probably they thought the Germans would never leave their Norwegian lairs in this weather. Kummetz followed the U boats' reports with close attention—*Only six to eight destroyers escorting,* they now told him.

Meanwhile tension was mounting in the chart room of the OKM in Berlin, as well as in the *Wolfsschanze* in East Prussia. During one of his last conferences, Hitler, who always loved figures, had made the generals listen to his calculations on the amount of munitions, weapons, cannon, and tanks which could be stored in the hold of a single ship, and explained how many battles they would have to fight in Russia to destroy the material which could be sunk to the bottom of the sea by one blow against a convoy.

There was indeed no question of victorious battles in Russia. The Eastern army was fighting on the defensive all along the line, the catastrophe of Stalingrad beginning to take shape. In view of the situation, the Oberkommando of the Wehrmacht (the OKW) [1] had addressed an urgent request to the OKM to make every effort to cut off supplies of weapons and war material on the sea route to Murmansk.

That was the reason why Kummetz was steaming with two heavy cruisers and six destroyers to meet the reported convoy on New Year's Eve, 1942. The prospects seemed promising, there was no danger of missing the adversary, whose escorting forces were outnumbered. . . .

On the morning of December 31 the news they had been expecting reached Berlin: a U boat lying in the immediate vicinity of the convoy signaled that German ships were in contact with the enemy, flashes of heavy fire from the German guns could be seen. It was to be assumed that Kummetz would first dispose of the British destroyers before tackling the merchant ships. Thanks to his superior gunfire he should have no difficulty in doing this. At least this was the view taken at the OKM, which was confirmed by further reports from the U boat—the squadron concerned, as was usual, refraining from breaking radio silence. Toward 11:00 A.M. the U boat reported:

Gunfire becoming louder—numerous ships burning—a red glow across the sky.

An hour later the first and only radio message was received from Admiral Kummetz himself. It consisted of three words: *Engagement broken off.* Consequently an extremely optimistic atmosphere reigned both in Berlin and at the *Wolfsschanze.* The words "a red glow" could only mean that the *Hipper* and the *Lützow* had set fire to one enemy ship after the other and finally sunk them, an entire convoy of war material—undoubtedly a big success. The year 1942, during which things had taken an unpleasant turn on more than one front, seemed to be taking its bow with a good grace after all.

In the course of the evening several visitors had already come

---

1 The supreme German command of all three services—as opposed to the OKM or Naval Command. [Publishers' note.]

to Hitler's headquarters to wish him a Happy New Year—Himmler, Ribbentrop, Speer, and others. Hitler was in a good mood. He told everybody that there was going to be a fine surprise, a gigantic convoy carrying war material to Russia had been sunk, a victory which he was going to make known to the German people and the world the next morning, New Year's Day, in a special broadcast.

In the meantime the hands of the clock were steadily moving on, and the nearer they drew to midnight, the more restless Hitler became.

"Why am I not getting a report from the ships?" he kept asking impatiently.

"Kummetz is on his way home; he must not betray his position by using his radio," the naval representative at headquarters, Vice-Admiral Krancke, replied. "As soon as he gets into harbor, we shall have news from him."

"When will that be, Krancke? When shall I get a report?" Inquiries were made in Berlin; the answer came that, judging by the approximate position of the engagement as reported by the U boat, the squadron was to be expected back early that evening. Still, that was hours ago, it was getting on toward midnight now, and still no report had come in. Naval headquarters remained silent. They just did not know if the ships had got back; in fact, they knew nothing at all.

They could not know that the *Hipper* had received a direct hit in one of her engine rooms, and that the squadron was limping home at half-speed; nor that a fearful blizzard was raging in the Norwegian fjords where during the night the ships had secured, interrupting communications with Berlin.

All this time Hitler's nervousness was increasing, and that night he was unable to sleep at all. Berlin had to be asked hour by hour what was happening, as with mounting impatience the Führer kept demanding news. But the OKM still remained silent: they had nothing to say.

Next morning the bomb went off. As the first day of the new year was dawning, Hitler had to listen to a special announcement from England instead of to the one he had planned. All Allied stations were broadcasting it:

"Great naval victory over superior enemy forces. Yesterday the Germans attacked a weakly escorted convoy in the Arctic with superior forces. The intrepid action of our destroyers under Captain R. St. V. Sherbrooke beat back the enemy. In the meantime the convoy has reached its port of destination at Murmansk without any losses. One German destroyer has been sunk, one cruiser severely damaged. The Admiralty regrets to announce the loss of the destroyer *Achates*."

After his first shock at this news Hitler's suspicions were immediately roused—not that he doubted the trustworthiness of the British statement, but rather that of his own admirals! He had the feeling he had been imposed on, that something was being concealed from him. He first vented his rage during the conference that morning—he still had received no report! His hands trembling, his voice barely controlled, he faced his officers and demanded they should telephone immediately to the OKM in Berlin, from his own table and in his presence.

"I demand an immediate report, this minute, do you understand? I demand they signal the ships telling them to report at once what went wrong. I am not interested if it's customary or not, and as to any objections the admirals may advance, they interest me even less!"

Raeder and his staff officers were equally furious. They knew that Kummetz must have his reasons for not sending a report. It was irresponsible to force him to break his silence before anybody knew what had actually happened. As telephone and telegraph wires were down, Berlin now sent out radio signals, but weather conditions in the north of Norway were such that even these were not received.

Still the signals kept going out into the void. At last—late in the afternoon—the first incomplete, partial report from the *Hipper* arrived. It was not calculated to mitigate Hitler's fury, or his sense of having been cheated. Admiral Kummetz merely reported that he had been forced to break off the engagement after setting fire to several enemy destroyers, because British cruisers had arrived on the scene and the *Hipper* had received a direct hit which had put one of her engines out of action. That was all.

Toward five o'clock Hitler was practically raving. At this most unusual hour, when he was accustomed to take a rest, Admiral Krancke was summoned to his presence. The Führer, who had not slept for nearly 40 hours, now proceeded to give vent to his whole disappointment over the big ships.

"I refuse to have anything more to do with them!" he shouted. "These ships are ridiculous; the moment one sends them out he is made to feel sorry for it and loses prestige. I tell you they're utterly worthless, more of a liability than an asset!"

It would have been unwise to attempt to interrupt Hitler's furious monologue. But his next remarks surpassed anything he had said yet:

"I have made up my mind, and I order you to make it known at once to your headquarters as my unalterable decision. The big ships have proved a waste of money, material, and men. They are to be put out of commission, scrapped, or smashed up or whatever you like to call it! I've had enough!"

This was too much for Krancke. Interrupting, he commented angrily:

"That would be the cheapest naval victory England ever won!" These words riled Hitler even more. He whom his propaganda had praised as the "greatest general of all time" strode up and down his bunker like a bull seeing red.

"I object to being put off with lies! The U boats with a few men sink more shipping in a day than the whole lot of battleships with all their colossal expenditure. I repeat, it is my irrevocable decision that the battleships and cruisers are to be put out of commission. Furthermore tell Grossadmiral Raeder I wish to see him here as soon as possible."

Admiral Krancke was still trembling with indignation as he telephoned what he had just heard through to Berlin. Two hours later Hitler received Raeder's reply: he was unable to come. He was sick. He was in bed.

This was actually true. The Grossadmiral had been so agitated that he had been forced to take to his bed. Moreover, it would have been quite pointless to argue about the use of a well-balanced fleet with a furious layman like Hitler. What did he know about the strategical advantages of "a fleet in being," of possessing heavy battleships whose mere presence near important naval areas forced the enemy to throw in all their available ships to neutralize the menace? What would Japan have to say about it if her German ally were to scrap his own ships and allow the British battle fleet to be sent to the Far East?

But all Hitler could see was the obvious fact that the ships had once again been unsuccessful. What he could not see was that he himself was to blame for the failure of the enterprise.

After the sinking of the *Bismarck*, the dictator, in his morbid anxiety lest anything should happen to his big ships, had given the order that on principle no big ship should be permitted to take the risk of going into action against an equally strong or superior adversary. Whenever strong enemy forces were to be expected, the German naval commanders were to avoid making contact. Over and over again, Raeder had vainly tried to have this principle overridden, which decisively impeded every operation.

As it was, the watchword "take no risks," and that only, had led to this new defeat. As soon as the *Hipper* and the *Lützow* were brought up against the reported convoy, Raeder had felt in duty bound to refer once again to Hitler's orders. Through his chief of staff, Admiral Fricke, he had reminded Admiral Karls in Kiel, under whose command these ships had been placed, of the order in question.

This had taken place during the night of December 31, when the ships were already at sea. Admiral Karls was rather annoyed. Every one of his commanders knew about the order; it was the same old story. Nevertheless, he tried to get through on the telephone to the Admiral in the north of Norway, in order to remind him of the order and give him the necessary explanations. But, as so often happened in the depth of winter, the telephone was out of order. The only way out was to send a radio message, which had to be brief. Still, it was better to be on the safe side.

Early next morning the Konteradmiral [2] in Altenfjord was shaking his head as he read the message: *Draw your attention to existing Führer's order, watchword "no unnecessary risks" must be observed when engaging enemy.*

That was obvious, thought the Konteradmiral; there was nothing new about that. But if in high quarters it was thought necessary to remind him of it, they must have their reasons. On the other hand, the ships would be contacting the enemy at any moment now. It would never do to worry Kummetz with long radio messages about something which was quite clear anyway. However, a short reminder could do no harm.

In the meantime, the *Hipper* had been giving trouble to the enemy convoy's escorting destroyers. Bravely as the British faced up to the heavy cruiser, they were no match for her 8-inch salvos. But at that moment heavy shells hit the water quite close to the *Hipper*—on the horizon flashes of gunfire were to be seen, coming from the British cruisers *Kent* and *Jamaica*, which had approached at full speed on receiving distress signals from the convoy. On the German side the second ship, the *Lützow*, which had been keeping at a considerable distance from the *Hipper*, was not even in sight.

The second British salvo achieved a direct hit in the engine room of the *Hipper*. The shell had pierced the armored deck while the ship, turning at full speed toward the new adversary, was heeling over to starboard.

At that very moment, a few minutes after the direct hit, Admiral Kummetz received the radio message on the bridge:

Take no unnecessary risks!

But at this moment the 8-inch guns of the *Hipper* and the

---

[2] German equivalent of Rear Admiral.

11-inch ones of the *Lützow* were roaring out together against the two English cruisers, for the *Lützow,* another so-called pocket battleship, had at last come up and at once gone into action. Unable to stand up to this unexpected fire of superior caliber from two different directions, the British were now doing their best to make their escape, greatly helped by the polar darkness, which in these short midday hours gives place to a pale twilight only, and by the dense snow blizzard.

In a minute the situation had changed. The British cruiser squadron had disappeared into the mist; there was no certainty as to its strength, and it might reappear at any moment. The low visibility did not permit the Germans to bring their superior gunfire to bear in order to keep the British cruisers at a respectful distance while at the same time detaching their six destroyers to attack the still weakly guarded convoy to the south. Kummetz was convinced that a success against the convoy, though certainly the primary objective, could only be obtained at the greatest risk. And at this decisive moment he held in his hand the piece of paper which meant so much—the signal which had just come in—*Take no unnecessary risks!*

One thing was quite clear, namely, that the message could only come from Hitler. And his flagship, the *Hipper,* had just received a hit which had reduced her speed to 17 knots . . . a situation precisely as covered by the Führer's general order. If he were to go after the convoy for even half an hour or an hour, the English might well succeed in bringing up heavy forces to cut off his line of retreat, now that he could not steam so fast, and so destroy him. . . .

So with a heavy heart Admiral Kummetz gave the order— *Break off action!*

Just as success was theirs for the taking, must they really let their valuable prey escape? For all the German commanders' astonishment, they had to retire without an explanation being given. And thus about an hour later the first and only radio message arrived from Kummetz: *Engagement broken off.*

The Naval Staff drew the only possible conclusion from this

signal, taken in conjunction with the reports from the U boat: the convoy had been destroyed, and a great success achieved. Hitler, too, spent New Year's Eve in a good mood in this belief. The great disenchantment was to come only on the morning of New Year's Day.

At the evening conference on the first of January, 1943, Hitler announced his "unalterable decision," which he had meanwhile committed to paper, for the scrapping of the German fleet, to all the officers present. Bellowing with rage, he now for the first time actually insulted his admirals, taunting them with cowardice in the face of the enemy in the same way as had become customary with him in dealing with his generals.

Grossadmiral Raeder knew that before Hitler would listen to reasonable arguments this fury must burn itself out, and with this in view he succeeded in postponing the decisive discussion for five whole days. He prepared his case carefully in advance, not thinking it possible that the Commander in Chief could actually confirm an order for the destruction of his own valuable fighting material. But the forces of opposition at Headquarters also had not been idle. Hermann Göring, one of its most influential figures, had long declared in his arrogant way that his Luftwaffe could easily take over the work of the *Kriegsmarine*. In the frequent bitter arguments on this subject between him and Raeder, Hitler had in the end always supported his old party comrade. In the belief that he now had a chance of giving a *coup de grâce* to his opponents, the latter convinced Hitler with detailed arguments that some of the best fighter and strike air squadrons at present lying around inactive in Norway in defense of Raeder's "tin boxes" could be effectively used in the defensive battle in the East. Apart from this he provided estimates for Hitler's benefit of the huge quantities of steel which could be saved for the armaments industry if the battleships, aircraft carriers, and cruisers were converted to scrap. He would just show these sailors how enemy convoys could be sunk with a single bomber squadron!

The duel between Hitler and Raeder started on January 6,

1943, when the first round consisted of a monologue by Hitler lasting an hour and a half, in which Raeder did not get an opportunity to interpose a single remark. Hitler began with the creation of the Prussian Navy, quoted the contributions made by the naval arm in the wars of 1864, 1870–71, and 1914–18, and declared roundly that in no single instance was success obtained. The Navy had always lacked determined fighting men, and the sailors' mutiny at the end of the First World War contributed much to the downfall of Germany at that time.

Hitler must have known only too well that what he had just, if somewhat exaggeratedly, described had always been a bitter thought in the back of the mind of the man sitting opposite him; he must also have known this was not the least of the reasons for the unprecedentedly audacious operations which the little German Navy from September, 1939, on, had carried through against a disproportionately superior enemy.

"This mutiny," Hitler went on, "and the scuttling of the fleet at Scapa Flow did not exactly add to the Navy's prestige. The latter was always particularly chary of committing itself, when there was ever any question of equality with the enemy in ships or men, an attitude which the Army has never shared. As a soldier I demand that once the order for action has been given the battle must be carried to a decisive conclusion. Battleships and cruisers cannot justify their usefulness any longer. Coastal Defense can make much better use of their guns than the 'tin boxes' can, and our armaments industry is crying out for scrap metal."

Yet this was the same man who had given the order for "no unnecessary risks" and upheld it in the face of all Raeder's opposition! Again emphasizing that his decision was irrevocable, Hitler now gave Raeder instructions to produce a memorandum in accordance with its provisions. "The opinion which you express in it will have historic value, and I shall check the document with the greatest care."

Now for the first time Raeder had a chance to say something in face of these heavy attacks. After sitting for some while immobile in his chair, he glanced up:

"I should be grateful, my Führer, for a talk with you alone."

Keitel and the other officers then left the room, and the second round began.

The following was subsequently reported by Raeder before the Nürnberg Court.

"I told him that I was asking for my resignation as I could see from his words that he was entirely dissatisfied with me and, therefore, this was the proper moment for me to leave. As always, he tried at first to dissuade me, but I remained adamant and told him that a new Commander in Chief of the Navy would definitely have to be appointed, who would have complete responsibility. He said it would be a great burden for him if I were to leave now, since, for one thing, the situation was very critical—Stalingrad was impending—and, secondly, since he had already been accused of dismissing so many generals. In the eyes of the outside world it would incriminate him if I were to leave at this point. I told him . . . if he wanted to give the appearance, as far as the outside world was concerned, that I had not resigned because of a clash, then he could make me a general inspector with some sort of nominal title, which would create the impression that I was still with the Navy and that my name was still connected with it. This appealed to him at once, and I told him on that day that I wanted to be dismissed on January 30, by which date I should have concluded ten years of service as Commander in Chief of the Navy under him."

But the third round of the duel was approaching, in which Raeder was to be on the attack, with, as his weapon, the memorandum which Hitler himself had required to be written. Day and night the innermost circle of the Naval Staff worked on this document, whose 5000 words, checked line for line by Raeder, was in its final form to become a fighting challenge. Part of it ran thus:

"The scrapping of German warships would represent a victory for the enemy toward which he would not have needed to make the slightest effort. It will cause rejoicing in the enemy camp and deep disappointment among our Allies, particularly Japan, and be looked on as a sign of weakness and of a complete lack of understanding of the supreme importance of the naval arm in the approaching final phase of the war."

Raeder pointed out that even those ships which were condemned to inactivity were tying down considerable British forces which could otherwise be employed in the Mediterranean or other theaters. The document reached its climax with the declaration: "Our enemy, England, whose whole conduct of the war stands or falls by the control of the seas, would regard the war as good as won if Germany were to destroy her ships."

Raeder's signature was one of his last official acts as Chief of Naval Staff. As his possible successors he singled out Admiral Karls, generally looked on in the Navy as the "Crown Prince," and the C.-in-C. U boats, Admiral Dönitz. Hitler did not delay for long and decided in favor of the man whose U boats had up to date sunk over 15 million gross register tons of enemy shipping; on him and on his U boats, which in spite of mounting losses were increasing in number from month to month, he from now on relied to attain victory over England.

Dönitz, upon whose U boats the Naval Staff itself had similarly placed all its hopes since 1939 and given them the heaviest task to perform, accordingly took over as Chief of Naval Staff. But just previously, on January 26, 1943, Hitler had in fact virtually sentenced the heavy ships to death. He had read Raeder's memorandum, it is true, but its only effect was to move him to make some more sarcastic remarks about the "Herren Admirale." His decision remained as unaltered after he had read it as before.

The order, which he now circulated to a small number of officers only "on account of the psychological effect," ran as follows:

1. All work in progress on heavy ships now building or in process of conversion is to cease forthwith.

2. All battleships, armored ships, and cruisers other than those required for training purposes are to be placed in reserve.
3. Naval personnel, workmen, etc., who become available as a result of this directive are to be employed with a view to accelerating the building and repair of U boats.

This order was presented to Dönitz, now Grossadmiral, so to speak as a christening present. Accepting this as a *fait accompli*, the latter was all the more keen to carry it out, for he promised himself a new and decisive impetus for the U boat arm from the releasing of thousands of officers and men and from the freeing of the whole of the dockyard capacity previously required for the big ships. It was only natural that a man who had reached his present level of success as head of the U boat arm should not see his new over-all responsibility from the broadest point of view. But the affair took on another aspect when Dönitz started work with his new colleagues on the Naval Staff. There the view was held that the remnant of the Navy still available must fail in its duty once such essential elements had been simply cut away from the whole. In the very first conferences it was put to Dönitz by his admirals that the battleship *Tirpitz* at least must be kept in commission even if it had to be disguised as a training ship. Dönitz was in any case already practically convinced of this—the scrapping hadn't after all got so very far yet.

Still the decision had to be faced shortly afterward when minds had to be made up over the future employment of the 31,000-ton battle cruiser *Scharnhorst*. On February 26, 1943, exactly a month after Hitler's "irrevocable decision," Dönitz was following up his objective at Headquarters in blunt enough fashion:

"I am convinced that the *Scharnhorst*, which has reported as being again ready for action, should be sent to reinforce our squadron in northern Norway."

Hitler was hopping about the room. What was this new man saying? Wasn't it only two weeks since Dönitz had handed in a scheme under which this same *Scharnhorst* was to be put into reserve on July 1?

"It would be a real triumph for England if . . ."

At that Hitler let fly. In an impromptu speech lasting half an hour he expanded, with manifold examples, on the uselessness of big ships, in an effort to convince the others and confirm his own decision. "Enough said now. Scrap them!" When he finally came to an end the Admiral took advantage of the momentary pause to remark drily:

"So, my Führer, I understand from what you have said that I can send the *Scharnhorst* to northern Norway."

Hitler gazed at him in astonishment. Nothing like this had ever happened to him before! What ought he to do now? Must he antagonize the "new broom" as well?

Finally Hitler gave way. Simply, with slight irony, "Do as you please, but think over my words later on, Herr Grossadmiral," he said. "I shall remember them all right!"

In this way the "unalterable decision" was reversed; it had been in force for just four weeks.

7

The "Ghost Ship" Coronel

For four years now Captain Ernst Thienemann had sat in Berlin in the OKM department responsible for shipbuilding. Since the war began it had been his task to supervise the conversion of German merchantmen into auxiliary cruisers. From his desk he had mapped out, so far as was possible, the voyages these vessels were to make, watching them put to sea with a heavy heart, while he himself had always to stay at home. There he had followed by means of meager and often uncertain reports their perilous track, as their commanders followed the trail of the ghost ships into the furthest corners of the seven seas.

There was Captain Rogge, who had been the first to go out with his *Atlantis* at the beginning of 1940, and who on a 622-day-long voyage sank 140,000 tons of enemy shipping before he himself was caught and sunk, in November, 1941, by the British heavy cruiser *Devonshire*, a few weeks before he was due to come home. Rogge and his crew did get back safely, however, on board a number of U boats. Before that, on May 8, 1941, *Pinguin*, under the command of Captain Kreuder, had been sunk in the Indian Ocean in an engagement with the British heavy cruiser *Cornwall.* Kreuder's successes were equal to those of the cruiser *Emden* and the auxiliary cruisers *Wolf* and *Moewe* in the First World War. Not only did he bring to account 120,000 tons of enemy shipping, but succeeded in sending 50,000 tons of it home with its precious cargoes of whale oil, wheat, and scarce raw materials.

The auxiliary cruiser *Kormoran* had a special success, when in a hopeless situation her commander, Captain Detmers, made a surprise attack on the vastly superior Australian heavy cruiser *Sydney,* and after a life-and-death struggle sank her. As the result of the terrible punishment she had received the unarmored *Kormoran* had to be blown up after her crew had been taken off. Again there were *Orion* under Captain Weyher, *Thor* under Kaehler and (on a second voyage) Gumprich, *Komet* under Eyssen, *Widder* and *Michel* under Von Ruckteschell, and— *Stier* under Captain Gerlach. In May, 1942, *Stier* was the last auxiliary cruiser to get unscathed out of "Fortress Europe," which the English were surrounding with a cordon, growing monthly more impenetrable, of ships, aircraft, long-range shore batteries, and locating devices.

Now, in January, 1943, Captain Thienemann surveyed the last three years—three years of German success, but three years, also, in which the enemy's defenses against this provocative form of warfare had become constantly more effective and comprehensive. Yet during all this time how much would Thienemann not have given not just to fit out auxiliary cruisers, but to sail against the enemy himself!

One morning in March, 1943, to Captain Thienemann's utter astonishment, an officer came up to his desk and said with a smile:

"Well, I'm your successor!"

"What?"

"Yes. My orders are to replace you immediately—you're getting a ship."

And so it was. The ship was the 5600-ton single-screw motorship *Togo* of the German Africa Lines. With her MAN engine she could do 17 knots. Thienemann fitted her out himself, using the latest devices and the experience of other auxiliary-cruiser commanders.

Ship 14—the official designation of the *Togo* as an auxiliary cruiser—had six 6-inch guns and six 4-cm. antiaircraft guns. She was also equipped with several 2-cm. four-barreled Vierlinger guns and machine guns—a respectable firepower; for, as the war developed, a ship in foreign waters was expected to defend herself against an increasing number of enemy aircraft. The auxiliary cruiser even had three reconnaissance aircraft on board—one ready for action on deck, the others in sections in the hold. The superstructure could be changed for camouflage purposes—the derricks shifted and the funnel enlarged; in fact everything possible had been devised to deceive the enemy. For the task of Ship 14 was to hunt, not to be hunted.

But would that still be possible in 1943? At first her commander gave little thought to that, being content merely to have a ship. Admiral Raeder reminded him of it when he came to report out.

"Thienemann," he said seriously, "this is our last effort with auxiliary cruisers; perhaps, if you are lucky and get through, the last but one. As long as we get results with this method we must go on trying—however much they step up their air reconnaissance."

From now on the captain began to appreciate the danger of his mission. He had to get through the Straits of Dover and the Channel. When, almost a year ago, the German battle cruisers had succeeded in passing through the Channel it had been hailed as an outstanding success. But what hope had *he* with his slow and vulnerable merchantman?

"The odds are a hundred to one," the Grossadmiral added, sensing what was passing through his officer's mind. "But if you really get through, it'll be easier 'out there.' And you won't be coming back here but will be going on to Japan. Good luck!"

On January 31, 1943, with a crew of 350, Captain Thienemann left the waters of Ruegen. Before that, he had thought out a new name for his ship, as every commander of an auxiliary cruiser had the right to. Berlin found no objection to naming Ship 14, *Coronel*—the scene of the successful battle of the German cruiser squadron in the First World War. It was in fact there, not far from the South American coast, that Thienemann's ship was to enter on her first field of operations.

Coronel sailed first to Norway to complete her working up in a fjord off Christiansand. The dash down the English Channel had to be made exactly at high tide. Otherwise, with her very considerable draft she might go aground in the shallow mine-free passage immediately under the Continental coast and make herself a sitting target for the English. It also had to be the night of a new moon. Everything had to work out to the hour if that hundred-to-one chance of a break-through was to succeed. . . .

It was here in this little Norwegian fjord, however, that the first delay took place. A courier brought an order from the Naval Group Command at Kiel: *Postpone departure 24 hours. Weather conditions do not permit sailing of convoy.* The captain was furious, for there at Christiansand the sun was shining out of a clear sky. Many an unkind word was spoken against the staff meteorologists at Kiel. Twenty-four precious hours lost, because they were having bad weather in Kiel!

Thus *Coronel* sailed 24 hours late, heading northward for the Arctic Circle. Only after dark did she alter course through almost 180 degrees, in this way hoping to deceive the agents who almost certainly had already warned London of the ship's departure and direction. In the Bay of Helgoland, however, she ran into a heavy storm which chased the floating mines in packs across the sea lane, and compelled the captain to put back to Sylt.

Finally, on February 7, 1943, after three more lost days, the *Coronel* embarked on the final attempt. Only a few men—old salts in civilian clothes—were to be seen on deck. The whole appearance of the ship was so changed that even the most suspicious eye would have taken her for a harmless neutral freighter. The crew of 350 had disappeared. But all the time a keen watch was being kept for the countless floating mines, which constituted the greatest immediate danger till they got within range of the British coast.

Suddenly a mine sweeper ahead stopped—it had run onto a mine, and only just succeeded in reaching Rotterdam with the help of tugs. Captain Thienemann had other worries besides this. Constant soundings showed only too clearly that the keel of his ship was gliding only a few fathoms above the sea bed. At short intervals there reached him the monotonous voice of the man at the echo sounder:

"Four—three and three quarters—three and a half. . . ."

All at once the voice rose:

"Three and a half—three—two and a half. . . ."

"Stop engines," the captain ordered, "full speed astern!"

But it was too late: a grating sound ran through the whole ship; she lifted slightly and the propeller lashed the whirling water ineffectually. The *Coronel* had run onto a sandbank and was aground.

Yet there was still hope. It was easy to see that only the bow had run aground while the stern swung freely. Moreover, it was not yet high water and there was a good prospect that the rising tide would lift her clear. Happily, after 45 minutes, the propeller pulled her at full power astern off the dangerous shoal and she was afloat again. There were looks of relief on the bridge. The treacherous spot was now given a wide berth and the *Coronel* sailed on toward the critical sandbank barrier before Dunkirk, sneaking along, hugging the land. But when Dunkirk was in sight the same misfortune befell her again.

This time the *Coronel* ran so hard aground that it was impossible to take any mitigating action—she was struck immovably. There could be no thought of getting her off, for at that moment the tide was ebbing. It would take at least eight hours before the water was high enough to lift her from the sandbank. Eight hours, every minute of which could bring a destructive attack on the stranded ship!

Meanwhile it had been seen from the shore that the *Coronel* had run aground. Before dawn broke, four mobile heavy anti-aircraft batteries took up their position on the coast under which the *Coronel* lay so close that they were hardly 300 yards away from her. This visible protection was reassuring, but could not really give much hope. What mattered more was that the weather was ideal for playing hide-and-seek: rain alternating with snow, mist, and limited visibility. Was it possible the British had not noticed this easy prey?

Yet once more the *Coronel* had the same luck it had had before at Christiansand, Sylt, and Helgoland. It remained unobserved, and this time right in the English fighter radius.

The following night the southwest wind, which had been driving the ship further and further onto the bank, veered to the northwest, and at high water the *Coronel* floated free without towropes. As the Straits of Dover could not be reached before light, she had to make a run for the harbor of Dunkirk. This meant a heavy responsibility for the commander. Would the English agents in Dunkirk send news of him just before he reached the critical narrows, even if he managed to keep his long daytime approach unobserved?

Meanwhile a pilot with local knowledge and a Luftwaffe R.T. operator had come on board. Slowly the misty daylight faded as the *Coronel* with her satellites, whose number had now been increased by 12 mine sweepers, passed Gravelines, halfway to Calais.

"Sir," the pilot called, "we are now within range of the Dover radar."

A minute later there is a flash to starboard—Dover's 16-inch guns!

"Gunnery officer! What is the time of flight?" the commander calls.

"Seventy seconds!" comes back from the gunnery director. Then, "Ten seconds—five seconds!"

The next moment eight huge columns of water rise up between the ship and its escort 300 feet out of the water. From then on for a full 40 minutes the Dover batteries hold the convoy, traveling at full speed ahead the whole time, in their grip. Yet not a single hit is scored.

Too good luck to last, thought the commander, as the ship made its way out of the inferno, its course now lying more southward. Indeed, there was little time to enjoy the luck they had had, for evidently the English were staking all on cracking this unusual nut. No old coastal steamer would be so heavily protected. Furthermore, British Intelligence in London would now be able to piece together the reports of agents and would know the whereabouts of the *Togo* (late of the Africa run) which had taken such a long time to fit out in Swinemünde. . . .

So the British posted a cordon of destroyers and torpedo boats, with cruisers waiting in the background, so that the fox should not leave its hole unnoticed and slip away to the wide Atlantic. The German radar promptly noted these suspicious maneuvers and notified the OKM. There could be little doubt that the English preparations concerned the *Coronel.*

While the reports of the movements of English ships were giving the commander a foretaste of what he might have to expect, suddenly the enemy aircraft alarm was given. Today, five days after new moon, the moon did not set until after 10:00 P.M., and even the young crescent illuminated the big ship well enough for the approaching bombers clearly to make out their target. Now, just as the antiaircraft opened up with a roar, a bomb hit her bows.

The effect of this was that the *Coronel* was forced to take her wounded to Boulogne for disembarkation and herself to run back to Dunkirk for repairs. Here, in attacks which grew more violent every day, the R.A.F. attempted to put an end once and for all to the raider as she lay in wait for the right moment to make her getaway. At the end of a fortnight she was struck by a heavy bomb which tore a great hole in her deck, but nevertheless failed to explode. Yet whether it was a delayed-action or a dud didn't really matter in the long run, for this hit resulted in the decision being taken not to send out the auxiliary cruiser again. Once more, perhaps, the enemy were to have a deception practiced on them when she slipped out of Dunkirk all right, not into the arms of the waiting warships but quietly back to Germany. There once more she was to spend many months in dock and be converted into a controlling vessel for Luftwaffe night fighters.

Although yet another even more modern counterpart of the *Coronel*, Ship 5, was later fitted with armaments, in practice this was the end of the war as far as German auxiliary cruisers were concerned. When Captain Thienemann reported back in Berlin and faced the new Chief of Naval Staff, Grossadmiral Dönitz shook his hand.

"I'm glad you got safely out of the tight spot," he said.

The captain remembered the parting words of his old chief: "The odds are a hundred to one." If that one chance had come off, the devil himself would have had to have a hand in it.

8

The Yellow-green Eye

THERE WAS NO NEED OF THIS PROOF—THE FAILURE OF the *Coronel's* attempt to break out—to persuade Dönitz that the main task of the Navy—the sinking of enemy tonnage—must now fall almost entirely on the U boat arm.

Since the spring of 1942 the U boat building program, which had been decided on at the beginning of the war, had been brought to the point that every day a new boat put to sea ready for action. In spite of the convoy system and increased Allied defenses successes had been mounting from month to month. But then, in the summer months of 1942, strange things began happening for which at first there was no explanation.

"We didn't know ourselves how it happened, sir. Suddenly a Liberator came through a thick cloud layer straight at us and dropped his charges. They couldn't possibly have seen us."

A U boat commander, just back out of action, was telling Dönitz of his experiences in the latter's headquarters at Kéroman near Lorient. This was Dönitz's routine with all his commanders. When they came in they were warmly welcomed, but next day at the latest they had to go through the mill of a full interrogation by their C.-in-C. which minutely covered every day, indeed every hour, of their patrol. They had to give an account of every order given, every decision made, every torpedo fired. There was no chance of glossing over a critical point, for Dönitz would at once ask:

"What was that? Just run over that again, would you?"

By this means he was in the closest personal touch imaginable with operational boats. He often told the officers of his staff that he could not hope to learn anything worth while from them, but he wanted to hear the opinion of even his youngest commanders, all of whom he called by their Christian names.

"Well, and what do you think about that, Hans?"

Every one of them knew he had to lay his cards on the table when he got home. There was no way out of it.

On this occasion the conference lasted the whole night. This was not the first U boat which suddenly, without previously having been sighted, had been attacked by an enemy aircraft. Up to date a thick later of cloud and above all the night itself could be regarded as safe cover for a U boat. Itself invisible, it could surface to charge its batteries or approach for a night attack on a convoy. But now the darkness which, above all else, had been the U boats' ally seemed to have turned traitor.

"We were surfacing at normal speed," another commander reported, "when suddenly we heard the noise of aircraft. A few seconds later a searchlight shone straight on our stern. Then he let us have it with his cannon. Obviously he hadn't been searching for us with the light, but must have known where we were in advance. The first beam came straight on our stern."

Dönitz and his officers brooded hard and long over this news, till finally:

"Well, enough for tonight," the Admiral said. "And you can go on leave. How long do you want? You can have my car to take you to the station tomorrow."

The Chief saw his commander to the door personally. When he came back his face was strained with the effort of trying to find an explanation for the inexplicable.

"Meckel!" He gripped one of his staff officers by the shoulder. "Meckel, what's happening? Attacks out of the blue . . . how is it possible?"

But Meckel didn't know the answer either—yet.

During the weeks that followed Dönitz harped back to the topic constantly.

"Maybe it's just coincidence," it was suggested.

"Coincidence!" Dönitz exclaimed irritably. "Don't you believe it. There have always been 'coincidences'—whenever the enemy has spotted our people before they've spotted him. In other words, the watch on the bridge has been asleep instead of keeping a proper lookout."

"There are too many reports of their surprise attacks to be just coincidences," another officer interposed. "The British aircraft must obviously have a new location device which lets them find their target even when visibility is nil."

"We have that too—radar."

"Yes, ashore and on board capital ships. But no one can mount such gigantic, sensitive apparatus with its reflectors and screen aerials on an aircraft."

This was getting no one any further. But the mention of radar decided Dönitz.

"We'll ask Maertens again; perhaps he's found the answer."

Admiral Maertens was the Chief of Naval Radio Intelligence. At the urgent inquiry by the C.-in-C. U boats as to whether the enemy's aircraft carried radar sets, he pricked up his ears. For some time his department had been on the track of this very question, and German radar stations along the French coast had been ordered to watch enemy radar activity on all possible wavelengths.

The first firm reports had already come in. At the beginning of June, 1942, Maertens sent Captain Stummel, who was later to be his successor, to Dönitz. After hearing the latest reports from the front, Stummel confirmed them:

"Yes, it is radar."

German stations had ascertained beyond doubt that British

aircraft over the Bay of Biscay were emitting high-frequency pulses while locating and approaching targets. But Stummel had more information than that.

"These instruments, called ASV by the enemy, work on the 1.2-meter wavelength."

There was nothing particularly new about this; the German *Seetakt* radar instruments operated on as little as .8 meters. But how did the British get these instruments into aircraft?

"Well, what can we do about it?" Dönitz wanted to know.

Stummel shook his head thoughtfully.

"One solution would be to install radar sets in all U boats. That would enable you to locate enemy aircraft in time to dive before you are attacked. But it would take some time. Not only that number of sets is not at once available, but from the experience we have had with experimental sets there would have to be improvements before they could work under the difficult conditions on board U boats. The other solution would be a radar detector. You wouldn't be able to locate the enemy exactly, but you'd know if someone was using radar in the area—and then you could dive."

"Would there be time to dive before the enemy could come up and bomb you?"

"I'm pretty certain of it, but of course only practice can prove it."

Cheered by this new hope, Dönitz straightened himself.

"I need these counterradar sets at once; better today than tomorrow."

Chance now came to the U boats' aid. Several hundred receiver sets which suited the purpose were discovered in a radio factory near Paris and were sent at once to U boat bases. They were simply called "metox," after the firm which had made them. Special antennae were improvised—cross-shaped aerials, not very large, which, as it was particularly over the U boat routes in the Bay of Biscay that British aircraft equipped with the new ASV operated, became known as "Biscay crosses."

Dönitz himself worked feverishly to have the boats fitted with the new defense devices as quickly as possible. He was worried enough. The enemy had sunk 12 U boats during July and as many as 15 during August, most of them by surprise attacks from the air. Never had losses been so high. Metox and the Biscay cross were going, or rather *had*, to bring salvation.

More good wishes and even higher hopes than usual accompanied the U boats which went their dangerous ways equipped with the new device. Right at the outset, in the Bay of Biscay, metox would show if it could really help. A few days later Dönitz gave a sigh of relief; the first satisfactory reports had reached him—metox had done the job.

It worked acoustically. As soon as the boat surfaced the Biscay-cross aerial was rotated in all directions. Below, a man sat at the metox with a headset, waiting tensely for the humming which was to betray the approach of an aircraft emitting radar pulses.

Pip-pip-pip, they would go, sometimes low and feeble, sometimes very loud and threateningly near.

"Aircraft!" the listener would shout up to the conning tower and at this magic word there was only one thing for all hands to do: get below and crash-dive! It was a matter of minutes, often of seconds, to dive to a safe depth before the aircraft reached the spot. This constant "Aircraft!" was an additional strain on the nerves—especially in the Bay of Biscay where the British no longer feared the Luftwaffe and maintained constant patrol with fast medium bombers.

But there were times when you just *had* to surface, the U boat commanders reflected bitterly. Under water the boats crept along at only three to four knots, and the batteries for the motors were soon run down. But as soon as you surfaced and set the Biscay cross in action, the man at the metox reported aircraft again.

In the neighborhood of the convoys it was especially bad. There it never stopped pipping and whistling because every destroyer, corvette, and aircraft in the area worked with radar, and you even heard the sinister *pip-pip* before the enemy set had located your boat.

Some crews became overtense, and the commanders themselves had had enough. They simply ordered the sets below to be switched off, preferring to rely on their eyes and ears than to live under this constant strain. But, of course, that too was only a passing reaction.

In spite of everything the C.-in-C. U boats could heave a sigh of relief. To be sure, his boats were forced more and more under water, and the struggle had again become one degree harder and greater in privations. But against the greatest danger—surprise by enemy aircraft—a counter had once again been found. Dönitz, however, was careful not to be overoptimistic. If they had circumvented one danger, no one knew what the next would be.

Consequently he never stopped sending memorandum after memorandum to the OKM in Berlin with warnings of possible sequels. At first, statistics proved the Biscay cross an effective remedy. In September U boat losses went down. Successes mounted. During November they sank almost one million tons of Allied shipping, their own losses being far outpaced by building, so that the number of "gray wolves" grew from week to week. On the other hand, enemy shipping was being constantly reduced, as their output could not keep up with the strain.

Thus, at the turn of the year 1942–43, Admiral Dönitz was at the peak of his success. If things went on like this, the Battle of the Atlantic could be won. But he had no illusions; he was worried. No one knew what was coming next.

About the time that Dönitz succeeded Raeder as Chief of Naval Staff, news arrived at U boat headquarters in Paris similar to that which had come in nine months before, in the spring of 1942. The staff was again faced with a riddle. Once more U boats were being attacked out of the blue, just as they had been before the introduction of metox. But now, even when they had metox, the enemy pilots were once more taking them by surprise.

In the meantime, much-improved radar search receivers had been fitted which swept the wavelengths automatically and showed a detection no longer by the nerve-racking *pip-pip,* but through a magic eye.

"Of course we had the metox on," a commander reported. He had been bombed a few hours after putting to sea by a British aircraft which dived at him straight out of the clouds, and had barely managed to bring his boat back to base. "But the thing was silent. I was starting to feel uncomfortable, because normally there is always something in the air in that neighborhood. I put on the headset myself. There just wasn't a sound. Almost at the same moment they were shouting 'Alarm!' in the conning tower. And before we could lift a finger the bombs fell."

As more reports of this kind came in, in most instances the outcome turned out not to have been so happy. The number of U boats which were not heard of again mounted frighteningly. However much Control called them, however much it radioed their call signals across the sea, the answer remained a deathly and all too significant silence. From January, 1943, on, more U boats were mysteriously lost from month to month. At the same time there was an increase in the number of radio calls from boats surprised by air attack without warning from their metox.

On February 8, Dönitz reported to Hitler that Allied convoys were being diverted around the positions where U boats lay in wait for them. The enemy obviously knew the exact position of the boats by a new location device.

"If we can't find some counter, I shall have to report that the U boat war is at an end."

For all this, the U boats did not give in. In a last great attack in March, 1943, they again achieved, despite mounting losses, results as high as any in the whole war. Over 60 boats attacked two big convoys between America and England. The battle went on for days, and for the last time the U boats were the victors.

In the following month, however, a group of U boats of similar strength was no longer able to get near a convoy. Under water they were much slower than the convoy, but as soon as they surfaced to use their superior surface speed they were detected at long range by destroyers and aircraft and had to dive again, unless they wanted to be destroyed within a few minutes. Finally the

"Black May" of 1943 brought the collapse of the U boat war. The list of boats which did not report back and therefore had to be presumed lost grew from day to day, until the month ended with a total loss of 43 boats. In the face of this terrible news Dönitz felt unable to take responsibility for what was happening and ordered most of his boats back.

The worst of it was that the Germans were entirely in the dark. It was known only that the enemy was snatching his prey with ghostly hands, but no one knew that these hands were an improved type of radar. One could guess that there must be altogether new location devices which enabled the Allies to "see" in all weathers while the U boats stumbled blindly into disaster. But this guesswork led to no certainty and, above all, to no effective countermeasures.

Again German radar units did all they could to solve the mystery. The first assumption was that the British had begun to use a different radar frequency after metox had made the 1.2-meter wavelength ineffective. But, however much possible wavelengths were monitored, there was not the slightest confirmation of this.

In the meantime new possibilities were discussed. Perhaps the enemy was working with thermal rays? Had he started to use infrared radiation to such effect that despite night, clouds, or fog, sea and ships lay as clearly before his technical eye as if they were in bright sunshine? All this remained conjecture. There was no proof.

But then something happened which could be proved. Several U boat commanders had always had an aversion to metox. This was not merely on account of the additional nervous strain, but the device itself made them feel uncomfortable. Radio operators sometimes intercepted curious noises when another U boat was in the neighborhood, and after they reached home it would transpire that the boat in question had been using its metox at the time. From this an obstinate rumor developed that metox itself radiated. And, if so, why should the enemy not make use of this radiation? Why should he not be able to intercept the metox radiations and fix the bearings and distance of their origin? Might not metox, devised to warn U boats, have become a traitor to them and a dangerous enemy?

Experts shook their heads. Of course the oscillator in the metox would give off some pulses; after all, anybody could "transmit" by coupling back any ordinary radio set. But an aircraft would have to carry complete laboratory apparatus to measure the metox's treacherous oscillations, if indeed they occurred.

However, the problem was tackled in the hope that perhaps after all here the solution lay. On a spring day in 1943 a single German aircraft, a Focke-Wulf 200, circled over the Gironde estuary while a U boat took part in the experiment below. *"Switch on metox!"* the signal came through to the boat's radio petty officer.

High up in the aircraft, a naval radio intelligence lieutenant, Von Willisen, watched his receiver. There, unmistakably, he could see the slight dip of the needle on his dial. In his headset too he could hear the metox working in the boat far beneath him.

"Tell them to switch it off," Von Willisen called, waving to the operator. The signal was passed down. Seconds later the U boat could no longer be heard. Several times the experiment was repeated until there could be no doubt: the metox did radiate. At 6000 feet the aircraft could hear the metox radiations of the U boat at a distance up to 110 kilometers!

The investigating party returned to Paris as fast as they could and reported the result to the C.-in-C. What happened now was typical of Dönitz. Within half an hour an order was teleprinted to all units concerned to rip out the metox immediately. Boats at sea received a radio call ordering them to stop using their sets.

The metox was radiating. So that was the explanation of the riddle, was it?

No. It was a fallacy. Not that metox radiated—that had been proved—but that the English had been using the radiation to locate U boats. Only too soon this was confirmed at sea, where the enemy continued to locate, surprise, bomb, and destroy one U boat after another whether they used metox or not.

In May, 1943, in one of the great conference rooms in the OKM building in Berlin there was suppressed excitement. The room seemed too small for the occasion, so closely packed was the audience of leading scientists, senior engineers of radio firms, all of them specialists in high-frequency techniques, high-ranking officers of the Luftwaffe and Naval Radio Intelligence services, of the OKM Operations Division and the U boat Staff. Grossadmiral Dönitz had called them together.

In addition there were some leading technicians from the Telefunken works. These men were on tenterhooks because of certain urgent work which was waiting for them in their laboratory in the Humboldt-Hain antiaircraft tower. There, protected by the yard-thick reinforced concrete walls of the flak tower, lay a small insignificant-looking object which even so was a technical marvel. Ever since January, 1943, when this instrument had been dug from a half-destroyed British aircraft shot down near Rotterdam, they had been trying night and day to reassemble it and to discover its secret.

On the dais stood a young naval officer from the staff of the C.-in-C. U boats, whose decorations proved that he had gained his experience in action before reaching his staff desk. With deliberate calm and objectivity he described what had been going on since the beginning of the year in the Bay of Biscay and in the Atlantic. He quoted the losses and made comparisons. And all the time between the lines could be sensed the unspoken phrase, "We don't know how it happens."

If they had not bombed us to bits in Zehlendorf, the men of the Telefunken works thought, then perhaps we should know by now; but at the beginning of March their works had been wiped out by a pinpointed air attack. Perhaps the English had guessed, perhaps even known, that here their secret was in process of being unraveled. As it was, the work of two months had been destroyed. Afterward when the remains of the instrument had been dug from the ruins, the technicians had moved to the flak tower, where the work of reassembling, experimenting, and testing had gone on afresh. But still the answer eluded them.

When the U boat officer had finished his report, Dönitz added a few words, the uncertainty and helplessness in face of the tremendous danger by which he was tormented plain to read on his face. His words now were such that none of those present would forget them in a hurry.

"Imagine what is happening," he said. "We send out five boats, a group with a single target. After a few days, all at once there are no more signals from them. They have simply disappeared without a trace. . . ."

Surely there must be an explanation, some means of countering this horror. As he finished speaking his voice had almost an imploring note:

"Help me, or the U boat war is finished. Give us some protection so that we can continue the fight!"

On May 31 Dönitz drove to Berchtesgaden and reported to Hitler in the Berghof about the situation.

"This month we have lost 30 per cent of our U boats which have gone to sea on operations. These figures are much too high. We shall be playing into the enemy's hands if we cannot avoid such heavy losses in the future. I have therefore withdrawn the boats from the North Atlantic into the area west of the Azores, where I can only hope the enemy air reconnaissance is weaker. As soon as the boats have their new armament and defensive equipment I intend to attack the North Atlantic convoys again. Above all, the boats need a receiver which can give them warning when they have been located by aircraft radar. But we have no receiver of this type. And we don't know for certain what wavelength the enemy is using to spot us, nor even whether he is using high frequency or some quite different locating gear, though we are doing everything we can to discover this."

A few weeks later a fortunate accident came to the assistance of the radio engineers who were working desperately in the Humboldt-Hain flak tower to reconstruct a British radar set.

Another similar half-destroyed set was salvaged from a shot-down aircraft, and at once dispatched to Berlin. It turned out that it had just those parts intact which had been missing from the first set, so that now reassembly was simply a matter of days. Shortly afterward, in fact, the technicians had gained their objective of being able to make the captured set work: and what they discovered knocked the wind out of them. . . .

Another gathering of leading German scientists and high-frequency technicians was summoned. These were the men who attended the monthly radar meetings held by General Martini of Air Intelligence and the members of the Navy's "scientific General Staff." They were practical men who had been trying to provide the fighting front with a means of defense against enemy radar ever since Dönitz made his appeal in May, 1943. Hitherto they had worked on surmise, quite in the dark. But from this day in August they would not be blind any longer, for they had at last come face to face with their unknown, technical enemy, and could look it literally in the eye. This eye was a large, slightly convex screen of opaque mat-surfaced glass across which a yellowish-green light flickered back and forth—the Braun tube. The experts attending this secret demonstration crowded tensely in front of the set, as a screen aerial above their heads described silent circles in the evening sky. From where they were standing on the highest platform of the Humboldt-Hain flak tower, blacked-out Berlin lay all around at their feet. Only here and there could be seen a faint gleam of light or the dim silhouette of a church steeple.

At this moment life appears in the mechanical eye before them. Bars and waves of light dance across the illuminated surface, then a dimly visible latticework like a spider's web. And then the picture gradually becomes distinct. Faint noises, a whisper here and there, are the only indication of the excitement of the audience. What they see moving slowly across the screen of the radar set in front of them is a faithful outline of the city lying in darkness around them. Not as distinct as a clearly defined photograph taken in sunlight, but sharp enough in its outlines and detail to render everything recognizable: streets, houses, the woods at the city limits. . . .

"Yes, that's the Müggelsee," someone breaks the silence at last.

"And that in front of it is the Zoo, and there's the Kurfürstendamm and the Gedächtniskirche," a second adds.

The impression was tremendous. Experts as they were, they all expected the enemy radar would turn the invisible into the visible, but no one reckoned with such clarity and panoramic effect. It was clear in a flash why it was that the enemy bombers could reach their target in any weather, and similarly clear why neither night, cloud, or fog could shield U boats from discovery from the air once they had to surface. The enemy sent out high-frequency pulses which were reflected back from every solid object they encountered in such a way as to give the outline, range, and bearing accurately to the operator looking through the "eye" of the radar set. And it emitted these pulses on the incredible wavelength of nine centimeters!

"So *that's* it!" some of the older radar experts told themselves, shaking their heads. "Centimeter wavelengths!"

Not that "centimeter radar," which the English developed into a perfected and decisive weapon, was completely unknown to the Germans or that they had never thought of the idea. It simply was that this line of research did not seem to them as promising as some others, a view which the experience of the first years of war seemed to support.

In October, 1934, a few men from GEMA, a private company, had carried out radar trials on the 48-centimeter band, on the Baltic coast near Pelzerhaken against the trial ship *Grille* which was steaming up and down for the purpose at some distance from the land. Tone reflections were used, and the ship was ranged on up to the respectable distance of 11 kilometers. It was just then that the idea occurred to them, instead of modulating, to transmit pulses and receive them again on their return, using the Braun tube. The Naval Command was horrified. "The Braun tube? That fragile glass thing? Quite out of the question.

A warship is subject to shocks, and it will use its guns. No, you must invent other methods of ranging, either that or a much more robust means of indication for the pulses."

Nevertheless, the Braun tube and the pulse method were worked out at that time and are now in use all over the world. The German trials showed superior performance, since elsewhere ranges of only from seven to eight kilometers instead of 11 were attained. On the other hand, accuracy of ranging in other sets was increased to a maximum error of 50 meters—an excellent achievement. But the decisive mistake was made in the autumn of 1935. GEMA extended their experiments into the centimeter band, which is in general use nowadays. Once again the constructors, engineers, and technicians intently followed the course of the *Grille*, steaming far away on the horizon. But the experimental 14-centimeter set gave no range indication.

Close the range! was signaled to the *Grille*. The ship steadily approached the shore—eight, seven, six kilometers. Still no reading on the centimeter set! It was only at a range of barely three kilometers that the Braun tube gave any indication. That was nothing. There was no need for a complicated technical instrument over ranges of only three kilometers—one's eyes were good enough for that. Yet at this decisive moment none of those who made their resolution were aware of its importance for the future. At the earliest stage of the centimeter trials the conclusion was reached which is accepted today, that these very short wavelengths produced purely optical reflections, as from a mirror. Decimeter waves, however, were more dispersed and therefore more favorable when reflected.

As a result, the centimeter experiments were finally abandoned, decimeter sets were developed and so well produced that at the beginning of the war the Allies had nothing as good as the 80-centimeter *Seetakt* radar sets in use by the Germans. The Allies had in fact taken the opposite path. In 1935, while the Germans were working on 14-centimeter waves, they had carried out experiments on 11-meter wavelengths and were subsequently impelled to go from these relatively long waves step by step to shorter and shorter waves until, in the middle of the war, they were in a position to master and turn to decisive use the special possibilities of the shortest waves of all—the nine-centimeter ones. This development had not remained entirely unnoticed by the Germans, however. When the airship *Graf Zeppelin* left on August 2, 1939, for a "visit of friendship" to England and flew for a noticeably long time along the coast of the British Isles, we were already on the scent. Churchill has written in his memoirs that the English coastal radar chain had the strictest orders to maintain radar silence during the airship's visit. So on her return the *Graf Zeppelin* was obliged to report that she had been unable to discover any signs of British radar activity, even though she actually had specialists on board, with radar receivers.

But this did not deceive the German Admiralty. It was known from other sources that the English had embarked on experiments using a high pulse frequency. We should have been only too glad to know what wavelengths they were using and how far they had gotten in their experiments. This was partially revealed in the early summer of 1940, when the Germans had pushed forward to the Channel coast and were able to observe the enemy sets at short range. The warning voices now became more and more numerous—it was not sufficient to be content with the successful results obtained at the beginning, but we must investigate much further into the still unknown realms of the highly important radar-ranging technique. We must know how to play on the high-frequency piano if we were not going to have some unpleasant surprises during this war.

Göring, however, refused to take any notice of these "ridiculous fears"—a contemptuous attitude which was summed up in his order to suspend all research work that could not produce useful results within the next six months! This was the period after the French campaign, the time of overconfidence, when Keitel, just promoted to Generalfeldmarschall, could actually say: "We've won the war. It's just that the rest haven't yet realized it!" Hitler himself issued the general order that no scientific research should be embarked on which could not be brought to a conclusive result within a year—a death sentence for any extensive research into new lines of radar technique. The Navy worked on, it is true, but only using a small group of technicians; while in England and America everything was being done to transform the inferiority of their radar technique by comparison with that of the Germans into a decisive superiority.

9

The *Scharnhorst*

IN 1943 THE ALLIES REWARDED HITLER FOR HIS SHORT-
sighted order, which had been responsible not only for the U
boat losses whose sharp rise had virtually brought the U boat
war to an end, but also for the loss of a battle cruiser which had
previously been considered one of the "lucky ships" of the Navy
—the *Scharnhorst*.

On the morning of February 15, 1943, a senior naval officer
was sitting waiting in the hall of the Hotel Adlon in Berlin
when a page approached him.

"Herr Admiral Thiele?"

"Yes?"

"The Herr Grossadmiral would like to see you."

A few minutes later Dönitz was shaking his visitor's hand.

"I want to speak to you, Thiele, about the possibility of using
the 1st Battle Group in North Norway."

"You mean the *Lützow* and the *Nürnberg*, Herr Grossadmiral?"

"Yes, but apart from them I consider it necessary for the
Tirpitz to go on operations once again. Finally, we must consider whether the *Scharnhorst* shouldn't be sent to North Norway as well, assuming I can get Hitler to agree to it."

"I believe that to be the only right thing to do."

The 31,000-ton battleship *Scharnhorst,* who fought a gallant battle before she was sunk in icy seas in 1943.

Hitler inspecting the 41,000-ton flagship *Bismarck,* sunk in 1941, during her first and last operation.

The HMS *Hood*, then the largest battle cruiser in the world, which blew up after a six-minute battle with the *Bismarck*.

The spray of a torpedo is visible at the bow of the *Bismarck*.

In 1945, the same ship, heeled over in Kiel harbor after a series of raids on the dockyards.

Grossadmiral Raeder, with mine-sweeper officers, who resigned as Commander in Chief in 1943 after a breach with Hitler.

Admiral Karl Dönetz, Commander of U boats, was appointed Chief of Naval Staff to replace Raeder.

Above, the heavy cruiser *Admiral Hipper*, safe in a serene fiord. In the picture below, the twisted guns and rents in the deck testify to the accuracy of the Allied bombs dropping on the Kiel dockyards.

During the early years of the war German U boat victories at sea ran high, resulting in the destruction of such vessels as an Allied freighter, above, and the HMS *Glowworm*, below.

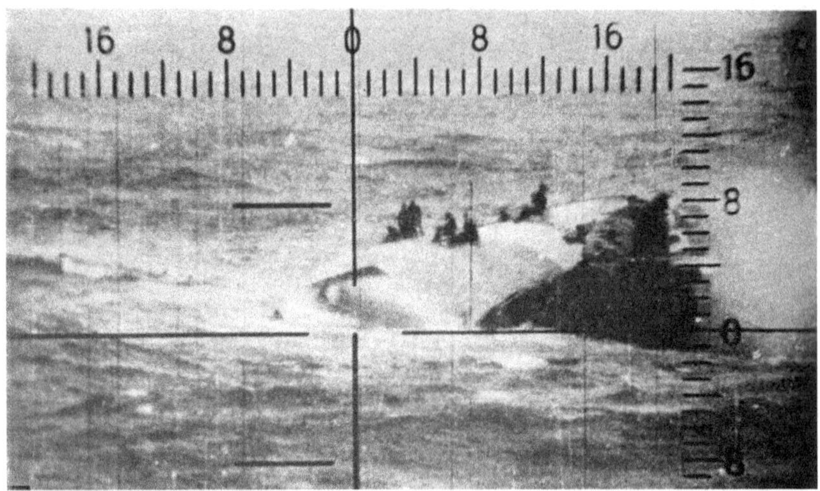

But when the tide turned, German U boat activities were restricted after heavy losses due to bombings and sinkings, as shown here. At lower right, survivors are being picked up by a sister U boat.

Above, the 10,000-ton "ghost ship" the *Admiral Graff Spee*, which was finally scuttled in 1939 outside Montevideo. The 6000-ton cruiser *Nürnberg*, below, was turned over to the Russians after the end of the war.

The *Scharnhorst*, above, plowing through choppy waters. Below, the *Scharnhorst, Gneisenau,* and in the distance the *Prinz Eugen,* during the Channel dash to safe northern ports—one of the most daring naval operations of the war.

The 10,000-ton cruiser *Prinz Eugen* rammed the 6000-ton *Leipzig* during heavy fog in the Baltic. For 14 hours the two helpless ships, inextricably locked, feared Russian attacks, which never came.

Above, the auxiliary cruiser *Togo* was converted to a night-fighter
control ship after she failed to break out into the Atlantic. Below,
a mine-sweeper flotilla clearing coastal waters.

Above, the one-man "beaver" and the two-man "seal" submarines. The Germans devised a camouflage for the periscope of the "beaver," below, that attempted to blow up the bridge at Nijmegen.

Midget submarines, like the "beaver" putting to sea above, were all the Germans had left in 1944 to harass enemy operations and supply lines.

Above is a submarine of Type XVII, the Walter U boat, with an underwater speed of 25 knots. Below, a typical German U boat bunker, this one at Trondheim, Norway.

The Type XXI submarine, above, and its "little brother" XXIII, below, are the streamlined electric U boats with which the Germans hoped to reopen the Battle of the Atlantic—but they were too late.

The 6000-ton *Köln*, above, firing offshore to delay advancing Russian troops, while the German Navy, below, rescued thousands of fleeing refugees from the Baltic.

"In any case I have just been able to obtain Hitler's full agreement to my intentions, that is, that the ships should no longer be subjected to such excessive precautions—at least pending their being sent into reserve. They will now be going out on operations, just as soon as a worth-while object and a chance of success turns up. The officer in command of a squadron sent to sea from now on will be able to act and fight entirely on his own initiative, without having to wait for special instructions from superior authority."

Thiele looked up in astonishment. The older circle of officers, which had much appreciated the cautious conduct of Raeder, had been somewhat skeptical of the appointment of the "U boat man," Dönitz, as the new Chief of Naval Staff. But when the latter was able to succeed in something for which Raeder had always worked in vain—the reversal of Hitler's "No risks" order for the big ships—this could only be welcomed.

"Well, that's a decisive point," he agreed. "It was always out of the question to fight successfully when you were bound by this crippling order."

All the same Thiele made no attempt to conceal his opinion that a breakout by the heavy ships into the Arctic would be dangerous. For now in winter the polar night up there allowed a few hours of twilight only, around midday. The fundamentals of sea warfare were only too well grounded in Admiral Thiele's experience, and with one of them he now raised a doubt in the mind of his chief.

"The risks of a night battle in those waters would be much greater for us than for the enemy, who in any case will have superior torpedo forces at his disposal, mainly destroyers and light cruisers."

"But I demand similar action from my U boats," interposed Dönitz, somewhat impatiently.

"The *Tirpitz* is no U boat, Herr Grossadmiral."

On that point in fact the two admirals failed to reach agreement. Thiele did go to northern Norway to take over command of the 1st Battle Group, but scarcely had he been two days on board the *Lützow* when he was reappointed elsewhere. Clearly he was not thought enough of a daredevil.

Meanwhile the relative strength of the forces in the north soon began to change. In proportion to Dönitz's success in reversing bit by bit Hitler's "unalterable decision" to put the big ships into reserve, so the advanced German weapon gained in strength and fighting power. Instead of the cruisers *Lützow* and *Nürnberg* of 10,000 and 6000 tons respectively, which were withdrawn, Allied convoys in the Arctic carrying vital war material to Russia now found themselves suddenly threatened by the 41,000-ton battleship *Tirpitz* and the 31,000-ton battle cruiser *Scharnhorst*. These fast modern ships, from their bases in Alta and Kaa fjords, could emerge at any time and deal painful blows at the main supply line for the Russian land front.

The "fleet in being" was back again! By this expression is meant that a fleet, by its very presence within striking distance of his lines of communication, can force an enemy to adopt extensive strategic precautions. He must, for example, even when his opponents do not attack, always keep superior forces in readiness for the occasion which may arise. The English, therefore, devoted all their resources to mastering so permanent a threat. On September 9, 1943, the entire German fighting group, consisting of the *Tirpitz, Scharnhorst,* and ten destroyers, carried out the successful Spitzbergen operation. But shortly afterward some gallant Englishmen succeeded in taking two midget submarines through all the booms and defenses into the *Tirpitz's* anchorage. Their special mines could not in fact destroy the great ship, but nevertheless they could put her out of action for a whole six months, which was what they did.

Now the *Scharnhorst* was alone the English could breathe again, for the situation had lost much of its menace. It could now be met by one superior battleship with a supporting force of cruisers and destroyers, with the consequence that the Admiralty decided to send bigger convoys than ever along the Arctic route to Murmansk. Meanwhile it had become winter again, and the conditions for operating the battle cruiser appeared even less favorable than when Admiral Thiele warned his chief about them. The ship must feel its way in the dark of the polar night. The secret of the British radar sets which had in the meantime been discovered made it quite clear that the enemy had the advantage of better gear than the old German radar sets mounted in the *Scharnhorst.* Moreover, from experience it was useless to expect support from the Luftwaffe, although it had established air supremacy in the sea areas adjacent to the Norwegian coast.

But meanwhile there were alarming reports coming in from the Eastern Front, where the German Army was engaged in savage defensive battles against the Russians attacking on several-hundred-mile-wide fronts. Each time a convoy full of American war material arrived in Russian harbors, its additional weight would be felt at the front a few weeks afterward.

This made Dönitz act. Whether the circumstances were favorable or not, he would attempt his utmost. He it was to whose face Hitler had cursed the *Scharnhorst* at the beginning of the year, and it was now up to him to prove that the ship still had a word to say.

A few days before Christmas, on December 20, 1943, the generals at headquarters listened to Dönitz as he made his report to Hitler: "Should there be any likelihood of a successful operation, the next Allied convoy in the north from England to Russia will be attacked by the *Scharnhorst* and her destroyer escort."

On Christmas Eve, 1943, there was a call through the *Scharnhorst's* loud-speaker system.

"Clear lower deck. Hands fall in on the quarter-deck!"

Everyone in the battle cruiser waited in suspense, knowing this was the "go," the order to sail on operations. Since noon the ship had been at six hours' and later at two hours' notice for steam. Now steam was up; the anchor might be aweigh at any moment. Never before had the crew laid aft so quickly.

"The Captain has instructed me to tell you," the first officer told the men, "that we are going to sea this evening for the destruction of an enemy convoy. According to reports a heavily laden convoy is now on its way to Murmansk. We must prevent its arrival there, and we shall in this way be helping our comrades on the Eastern Front who are at this moment engaged in one of the heaviest battles of the war."

Later, when the ship was already under way, a signal was received in which Dönitz set out the problem in brief terms: *Make bold and skillful use of the tactical situation. The fight is not to be half finished. The superior gun power of the Scharnhorst is to be used, and destroyers sent in to the attack. Use own judgment in breaking off action. Important to do this on encountering superior forces. Ship's company to be informed in this sense. . . .*

The men in the destroyers called their old commodore "Achmed Bey." He was Konteradmiral Bey, who, as senior officer, was in command of the operation because the actual flag officer of the 1st Battle Group, Admiral Kummetz, with his Chief of Staff, was on leave subsequent to the damaging of the *Tirpitz*. The staff had approved their going quite happily, for it had seemed unthinkable to send the battle cruiser to sea in the deep polar night. But as it was, it turned out otherwise—with the result that this difficult operation was in the charge of an officer who had never commanded a battleship, although he was a well-known destroyer commander.

To begin with, everything went as well as those on board could wish. The convoy—whose official title was J W 55B—was several times sighted and reported by German forces in spite of bad visibility, night, and snowstorms. Long-range reconnaissance aircraft picked it up with their radar, and U boats were stationed on a wide arc of reconnaissance across which the convoy must pass to reach its objective. Having allowed the convoy to pass, they surfaced and immediately reported its position. From all these reports the staff could get an approximate picture of its course. And *Scharnhorst* and her five destroyers were steering at high speed toward the estimated point of contact.

In the early-morning hours of the second day Konteradmiral Bey ordered the destroyers to carry out a wide sweep to the northward. At first the *Scharnhorst* remained astern of them, but then turned onto a northerly course and was soon out of sight. The destroyers never saw the battle cruiser again. Only once afterward, at about nine in the morning, they made out star shells in the sky in the direction in which they believed the ship to be. Was she in action?

According to Chief Petty Officer Gödde, one of the survivors, who was standing during the whole action quite close to the conning tower in his action station at the port captain's sight, it was exactly 8:24 A.M. when he suddenly saw great columns of water through his binoculars.

"Those are shell splashes," flashed through Gödde's head, "from medium-caliber guns!" He reported at once to the captain on the command telephone line, with which he was connected: "Several splashes, estimated to be 8-inch, 400 to 500 yards on the port side."

At this moment the first star shell burst into brilliant light through the thick snow squalls, slightly to the side of the German ship. These were being fired from another direction—there must be several enemy ships in the vicinity, probably cruisers, and they had sighted the *Scharnhorst* without first being picked up by her. In this way they had been able to train their guns quietly on an enemy who could not see them, blind as she was in the darkness of the snowstorm.

"They can only have done that with radar," thought the German captain, Captain Hintze. Aloud he asked, "No report from the radar set?" The report came through at the same instant, just as the second salvo from the invisible enemy crashed into the water, dangerously close now to the ship. At last the foremost radar set has picked up the enemy. Meanwhile the gun directors have trained onto the enemy's bright muzzle flashes, firing out of the misty distance—the only point of aim which all their efforts can find. And seconds afterward the first salvo crashes from our own main armament.

But there lingers an unpleasant feeling, most of all among those who realize the importance of this early and accurate radar ranging by the enemy in such conditions of weather, when visibility is practically nil. And this feeling is heightened when, after the 15-minute action which the German battle cruiser breaks off through her high speed, taking advantage of the fog, there is a report concerning the single hit received—it has passed through the foremast. The radar has been hit and is no longer in working order. . . .

"That *would* happen," the captain observed, "and in weather like this!"

"All the same, Hintze," the senior officer replied, "we must make another attempt to get at the convoy. We are now steaming north, and we'll come in from there. By that time, with luck, we shall have shaken off the cruisers."

"That's it—we shall have to rely on the after radar set, although it's not placed so high and can't operate ahead."

The clock in the charthouse of the British battleship *Duke of York* was showing 03:39 on the morning of December 26 when a flag lieutenant approached Admiral Sir Bruce Fraser where he was sleeping in a chair.

"Signal from Admiralty, sir."

The Admiral was awake in a moment, and he had scarcely read the few lines of the signal before he had sent for his Chief of Staff.

"Well, I was right," he began. "The Admiralty has just reported that the *Scharnhorst* probably went to sea yesterday evening." The Chief of Staff crossed to the chart on which was indicated the position of all British ships at sea, of the valuable convoy, which was escorted only by destroyers, of the 10th Cruiser Squadron, consisting of the cruisers *Belfast*, *Sheffield*, and *Norfolk*, and lastly of his own battle squadron, consisting of the

35,000-ton *Duke of York*, the cruiser *Jamaica*, and four destroyers. A quick glance was sufficient.

"If the *Scharnhorst* attacks at once and then disappears again we shall not arrive in time, sir."

"That's correct. Clearly we shall have to steam east at high speed so as to cut off her retreat."

"If the cruisers can bring her to action and stop her, we may perhaps do it, sir."

"There's one other possibility. The *Scharnhorst* is certainly making for the convoy. She'll want to avoid action with our cruisers if she possibly can. So the 10th Cruiser Squadron must remain between her and the convoy so as to keep the *Scharnhorst* at bay. We shall turn the convoy itself onto a more northerly course so as to draw the *Scharnhorst* further away from the coast."

"For that we shall have to break radio silence, sir."

"Yes, that's true. The Germans will know we are approaching. But in the long run that is the lesser of the two evils, and it must be accepted. I only hope that once the cruisers have made contact with the *Scharnhorst* they will be able to form a consecutive picture of her movements with their radar."

And that was exactly how it happened. Through their radar the English were in a position to shadow the German ship and to attack it when it approached too close to the convoy. In the first engagement of this kind, as we have said, the single radar set on the foremast was destroyed by the only hit she received, other than a shell which did not explode. And again on her attempt to pick up the convoy from the northward while the detached destroyers attacked from the south she came up once again against the cruisers, waiting vigilant as watchdogs.

During this whole period, as the convoy made a skillful detour to the northward, Admiral Fraser, far to the west, pressed on at full speed with his heavy battleship in order to close the pincers around the German ship.

About two hours after the first engagement with the British cruisers a radio message was received in the *Scharnhorst* from

Gruppe Nord. Admiral Bey knitted his brows. An air reconnaissance report referred to a formation of five ships to the west of North Cape. The position given was approximate.

"Well, they can't be German ships; we would know about them all right," the Admiral said to Captain Hintze. "It smells to me unpleasantly like an enemy force which we haven't yet heard about."

"Five ships—probably one or two battleships with screen, Herr Admiral."

"I think so too. Well, we can't do anything for the time being; they are much too far to the westward. There's nothing for us to do except go for the convoy!"

The OKM had assumed that the aircraft had sighted our five destroyers returning to base. They guessed therefore that Admiral Bey had detached the small ships on account of the storm and heavy sea. For this reason they gave Bey no further instructions, as they would certainly have done in different circumstances. The conduct of the Senior Air Officer in the Northwest had also contributed a good deal to the confusion. In fact the first aircraft report ran as follows:

Five ships probably including a heavy ship sighted northwest of North Cape.

The Senior Air Officer had met the observer concerned with a sharp remark on landing.

"I don't want to read any 'probable' information in reconnaissance reports from here. You are simply to report what you have seen!"

So "probably including a heavy ship" was left out. If it had stayed in the message, the OKM could scarcely have jumped to the conclusion that the message referred to our own destroyers. It would then not have repeated it without comment to the *Scharnhorst* but would undoubtedly have given an urgent warning about the approaching English battleship.

Well, that did not happen, yet in fact Admiral Bey made a correct evaluation of the situation nevertheless; he knew quite well that the five ships which had been reported could not be his own destroyers, which he had not yet released. But as a result of the approximate position given he considered the danger to be possibly further to the westward than it actually was. There was nothing to do now but to go for the convoy—and by this means he was drawn even further northward and away from the coast. When he finally realized with a heavy heart, after a second engagement with the radar-watchful cruisers, that he would not be able to reach the precious transports in this way, it was too late, and he gave orders to break off action.

In the meantime Admiral Fraser had put his force into the gap, and the pincers were closing. At any moment the radar sets in his flagship the *Duke of York* might report picking up the *Scharnhorst,* which was still being held continuously by the radar of the shadowing cruisers. At a time when normal eyes aided by the best binoculars could make out nothing but darkness swept by ghostly snow squalls, the yellowish-green eye of war was controlling this fight as well.

The book by F. O. Busch, *The Tragedy of North Cape,* taken from Admiral Fraser's official report and from the accounts of the few German survivors, describes how the *Scharnhorst* ran into an enemy bent on her destruction, and how she carried the unavoidable fight, herself almost blind against an enemy who could see through his radar, through to the bitter end. Shattered by heavy shells and hit by countless torpedoes the *Scharnhorst* finally capsized at about 7:00 P.M. on December 26, 1943, to sink a short while afterward into the icy sea. At that moment hundreds of survivors who had got out of the ship in time were still swimming, struggling with all their strength to keep themselves above water, on to life rafts, wooden gratings, anything which would float. But their limbs soon stiffened from the cold and their strength left them. That was how most of them, including the Admiral, the captain, and all the officers, were swallowed up before English help could arrive.

Two British destroyers between them saved 36 German seamen, but over 1900 went down with their ship.

At this time Admiral Sir Bruce Fraser summoned the officers of his staff and of his flagship, the *Duke of York.*

"Gentlemen," he said, "we have sunk the *Scharnhorst.* This is more than a victorious engagement; it is a strategic success of great importance: the 'fleet in being' of our enemy, the threat to our convoy route, has ceased to exist. There will be other tasks for us next year." The Admiral glanced silently along the line of officers, before raising his voice. "There is one thing more that I should like to say, gentlemen. If you should ever be in the position of having to command a heavy ship against many times superior odds, I hope that you will do as they did, that you will maneuver your ship as well and with your ship's company will fight as bravely as the officers of the *Scharnhorst* have done today."

When the *Duke of York* sailed next day from Murmansk to England, Admiral Fraser had a large wreath dropped over the side at the position where the *Scharnhorst* sank. There with his officers and the guard of honor he stood long at the salute, while in final greeting the English wreath sank slowly into the German seamen's grave.

10

The 3rd Mine sweeper Flotilla

WITH THE SINKING OF THE SCHARNHORST THE GER-mans had, at the beginning of 1944, no battleship left which was ready to go into action. The U boat arm, too, was as good as paralyzed. Forced under water as they were, the boats had, paradoxically enough, lost their mobility. With their batteries only giving them the power for a few hours' underwater journey, they had become unwieldy, slow "lame ducks," as Dönitz called them. With their own losses risen to more than 50 per cent of the total employed, their achievements in terms of sinkings, compared with those of 1941 and 1942, were small enough in all conscience, and their employment was justified mainly by the costly and otherwise wasteful defense system which the British were forced to keep up.

Under these circumstances only the true submarine could help, a boat that could be really swift and powerful under water. Something of this kind had already been constructed and tried out, and its mass production was being pushed ahead with all the means still available to Germany in the winter of 1943–44.

When we speak of the Navy it is obvious that it covered the

U boats and capital ships. People are also aware of the destroyers and E boats, and of the auxiliary cruisers, whose journeys had the glamour of far adventure. But how many think of all the little ships of the Navy off all the coasts of Europe—the mine layers and mine sweepers, escort vessels, submarine chasers, patrol boats, the harbor-defense craft, and auxiliary vessels of all kinds, which, manned by German sailors, fulfilled their numerous guard and security duties as part of Germany's defenses? Many of their crews went to sea in nutshells, in any old tub, in harbor boats capable of mounting only a 20-mm. gun.

Yet these men were the mass, the infantry of the Navy. It was they who made it possible for the others, whom we know better, both to put to sea and to come back to harbor. It was their duty to guard the convoys and the coasts, night after night on patrol, by day searching the sea lanes for mines, and always competing with the growing superiority of the enemy air force. Such were the "little men," whom scarcely anybody mentions when speaking of the Navy. And yet they belonged to it; they were part of its struggle and defeat.

One story here must stand for all: the story of the 3rd Mine sweeping Flotilla.

It begins strangely enough. The Third motored—by road—to meet the enemy, in this case the Russians on the Black Sea front. On great 64-wheel load-carriers the 120-ton boats rolled slowly southward down the Autobahn from the banks of the Elbe near Magdeburg. When they reached the Danube they were launched into their own element, to continue down the river under their own power. By the same route (the only one) to the Black Sea, there followed E boats, ferry lighters, and even small U boats. Some idea of what they sailed against may be gained by considering Russian naval strength in the Black Sea, which comprised several cruisers, destroyers, and gunboats as well as many small craft whose fighting power was roughly equal to that of the Germans, and, in addition, several submarine flotillas. . . .

However, it was soon apparent that the Russians did not

know how to use the superiority of their Black Sea fleet. Besides, it was still the time of the German advance, and the Stukas several times successfully dive-bombed the Russian ports in the Caucasus where the fleet was lying. Only the enemy submarines showed an increased activity.

Meanwhile the Third was carrying out its many tasks, which were by no means confined to mine-sweeping. Demands of all kinds on the small group of little ships could not have been greater. There in the Black Sea the flotilla not only had to guard transports and convoys; it also supported the Army fighting on land, moved forward with its advance, assisted in the land battles, and bombarded enemy positions such as the "death mountain of Novorossisk." When ammunition was all but used up and superior Russian warships appeared, retreat was the only means of salvation.

But there are times when mine sweepers have to stay close to the enemy, even when his fighting power is ten times greater. In 1943, when the Russians were gaining final superiority on land, it was the little mine sweepers' job to support the retreat of the German troops as best as they could, as they had covered their advance.

In November, 1943, the enemy felt strong enough to push thousands of troops across the wide Kerch Straits to the Crimea, thus forming the first bridgehead on the peninsula, which was still in German hands. Their first assault went well enough. But the Russians had a chance of final success only if, masters at improvisation as they were, they could bring, night after night and with every floating means they had, reinforcements, supplies, weapons, ammunition, and, above all, fresh water, across the straits.

The German Black Sea "fleet" received orders to stop the passage of Russian supplies across the straits, to strangle the flow at any price in the hope that the weak troops on the Crimea would then be in a position to expel the Russian forces in the bridgehead. "Fleet" was a rather high-sounding name for the forces the Navy had at its disposal—the mine-sweeper flotilla, a few E boats, and a flotilla of lighter ferries and Siebel ferries. On the Russian side there were hundreds of craft of all kinds including the heavier gunboats and destroyers. But their range was limited by two factors. For one thing, the Germans had blocked the straits with mine fields in such a way that the mine-free passage was extremely narrow; and secondly, the Germans forced their way right in among the Russian transports in such a fashion that the latter could hardly use their superior artillery without damaging their own side.

In this way, within a few nights, German warships—this fleet of nutshells—established a kind of command of the sea in the Kerch Straits. This was achieved by something virtually unique in modern naval warfare—a nautical street fight, waged from nutshell to nutshell, man to man, during which, as often as not, the opposing ships shaved past each other with only yards to spare.

During the night of November 7, 1943, our mine sweepers pushed for the first time in this hand-to-hand fighting into the straits, and passed the mine barrier, groping carefully forward in the darkness. If it was true that the Russians kept up a lively ferry traffic across the straits, contact would be made at any moment.

"Object to starboard," a number of lookouts reported at the same time.

"There they are!"

Already our ships were right among the enemy. The Russians had put to sea with everything that could float, hurrying across in ferries, small steamers, motorboats, tugs and lighters, barges, and even rowboats, canoes, and makeshift rafts.

"Switch on the searchlight!" ordered the flotilla commander as soon as he was aware of the situation. "See we're not grappled!"

It was the days of piracy again. Many of the men must have been reminded of pictures of the great naval battles of the past, in which opposing fleets sailed close enough to fire broadsides into each other's hulls. The opponents faced each other at pistol range, the hand-to-hand fighting lit up in ghostly fashion by the tracer bullets, searchlights, and star shells. The battle was hot, but the Germans, with their faster and more maneuverable boats, kept the upper hand.

On the second night the Russian gunboats were lying in wait, intending not only to keep their dangerous enemy at bay but to blow him to pieces with the superior range of their guns. But these could not be depressed below the horizontal, and so could not fire lower than deck level. Taking advantage of this, the German commander gave orders to approach so close that his boats should run under the trajectory of the Russian shells.

This was accomplished. Soon the enemy gunboats were lying close enough to touch, with the Russian artillery firing ineffectually into the sky. Our men, on the other hand, had brought a surprise with them. They had borrowed some multiple rocket-launchers from the Army and these "Stalin organs" they now trained on the Russian ships. Others raced at full speed for the gunboats, swerved at the last moment, and lobbed depth charges beneath the enemy's bows.

Shortly afterward the "street fighting" started again with another attack on the Russian supply route, in the course of which the 3rd Mine sweeping Flotilla constantly invented new methods of defense against superior forces and of cutting the life stream of the Russian bridgehead. For example, they sailed so close to the somewhat larger enemy ships that with a line-throwing pistol they could fire across a line to one end of which an iron hook was fixed, intended to hold fast somewhere on board the enemy; at the other end there was tied an explosive charge which was slowly drawn by the line against the Russian hull. (That is, if things went according to plan—in some cases they really did.)

The Russian losses were very high. Their High Command was said to have offered a reward of 50,000 rubles for the capture of the German flotilla commander. But the commander was not cooperative. After a few nights, control of the Kerch Straits was established. On November 17 army units attacked and shattered the Russian forces in the Crimea, weakened as they were through lack of essential supplies, and the bridgehead was wiped out.

The following year, 1944, however, brought both the collapse of the German Eastern Front and the end of the naval units in the Black Sea. The Crimea front was turned from the north by the sheer numbers of the Red Army. On their last missions the mine sweepers helped to evacuate the main body of German troops from Sevastopol to the Romanian and Bulgarian coasts, from which the soldiers moved off as quickly as possible. As many as 450 men were crowded on board the mine sweepers on these last voyages and the little vessels were weighed down by this extraordinary load till their upper decks were level with the water. Finally the last hour struck for the 3rd Mine sweeping Flotilla. On August 28, 1944, the Germans scuttled their ships off the Bulgarian port of Varna and allowed themselves to be disarmed on land by the Bulgarians. The flotilla commander, however, had provided himself with a document, signed by a well-known Bulgarian general and embellished with impressive seals. "The German naval officer Kapitänleutnant Klassmann and the 800 men with him are hereby authorized to have free passage and an escort to the Bulgarian border."

This might work with the Bulgarians, but how about the Russians, who were reported already to have taken the center of Sofia with parachute troops? Our sailors sneaked cautiously around the Bulgarian capital. There was no life in the railway yards—would it be possible to get a train? There were cars enough. And within two hours two chief petty officers came riding in on a locomotive; they had managed to persuade a Bulgarian railwayman, who knew a little about the job, to drive a train to the frontier. This journey, which later, when the Bulgarian made off with the locomotive, turned into a route march from the Black Sea to the first German positions in Yugoslavia—all through enemy-occupied territory—was one of the greatest wartime adventures of a German naval unit. With their "armored" train—minus locomotive—they rumbled down a hill-side into the Yugoslav frontier town, took the station by a *coup de main,* and there fitted themselves out for the rest of the journey. An order to capitulate, issued by the commander of a strong unit of Tito's partisans, was answered by a threat to shell the town and his positions unless they were guaranteed safe transit. At the same time gun barrels (a battery of telegraph poles) were elevated menacingly above the sides of the open flat cars, being swung with artistic effect on the sailors' backs. In fact, there were only two pistols among 800 men.

Finally they were able to capture a radio transmitter and make contact with the German lines. They received the reply that a motorized unit would come to meet them. That was how the crews of the Third, after a 300-mile march through the Balkans, came to be met by half a dozen trucks with German infantry amid the rugged mountains and valleys of Yugoslavia. These last were Austrians, and they shouted their greetings in broad dialect:

"Well, and who are you?"

The sailors were at no loss for an answer.

"Russians, can't you see?" they called back.

"Well, fancy that: the Navy marching." The Austrians shook their heads. "Don't you know it's dangerous to go hiking in this country? The mountains are full of Titoists—keep your eyes open. We'll cover your rear."

This handful of soldiers was never seen again. They were probably smashed by Tito's advancing units. When the sailors heard of this in Nish, behind the German lines, they swore they had been saved only by their singing. Klassmann had ordered his 800 to sing marching songs and chanteys as loud and long as possible to give the impression of large numbers.

In Nish they found a radio message from Admiral Dönitz: *Return to Germany as quickly as possible for re-formation of 3rd Mine sweeping Flotilla.*

This they did. As soon as their new boats were ready, though still without their full armament, they were put to evacuating refugees in the Baltic. Then came the capitulation, and once more Kapitänleutnant Klassmann came into contact with the Russians.

It was after the war at Swinemünde, where he had taken his flotilla to surrender it. The Russians had insisted from the beginning of their negotiations with the British that they wanted the 3rd Mine sweeping Flotilla at any cost—with the original crews. Rumors of these negotiations had reached the men. And although the English gave an assurance that there would be no question of their being handed over, the original crews were successfully smuggled away and slowly replaced with others.

The Russians, of course, won their point, and the flotilla was handed over. But the crews were scattered to the winds. Only the flotilla commander was willing to take a risk, just for the hell of it, and insisted on going with his ships. At Swinemünde he got a British military policeman to escort him, seeing he was determined on going ashore. He had hardly set foot on the jetty when some Russian officers approached him.

"Where did you leave your men, Commander?" they asked.

They must have been fully informed, because they mentioned names. But they were not angry or distrustful. Instead they were smiling. And with a jerk of the head toward the military policeman, the speaker went on:

"Do not be afraid. War over—all forgiven and forgotten."

Then Klassmann realized what they were after. They wanted him and a few others as instructors in Russia.

"Come to us with your men—you'll do all right."

It is known that others accepted such offers, mainly because their families lived in the Russian Zone, and it is also known that the promises made to them were kept. They were attractive promises—good pay, good quarters, assistance for dependents in Germany. But Klassmann refused.

The ships of the Third sailed east, like so many other German warships, but without instructors. Today their fate has been fulfilled and they are part of the Soviet Navy.

11

Torpedo Boats

THERE WAS NOTHING PARTICULAR TO REPORT ON THAT evening of June 5, 1944. The night came down over the French Atlantic coast rather cool for the time of year, and the German soldiers on guard on this sector of the Atlantic Wall (a questionable defense against the British) felt a little chilly.

At the naval headquarters, Gruppe West, in Paris, all-quiet signals were coming in from the radar stations. For there, too, nothing out of the ordinary had happened; the daily attacks of the R.A.F. on their installations had become routine. The British would come during the early evening, before dusk, flying low across the sea and then shooting suddenly and unexpectedly out of the red disk of the setting sun.

But these surprise tactics made little difference. German radar detachments were only too accustomed to their daily "visitors" who would have liked to put out the eyes of the German radar with their rockets. They scored some hits indeed, but the most valuable and sensitive parts of the radar instruments were stored safely below, deep in the bunkers, against the moment when the raid would be over and they could be returned to their sets.

That was how it had been for months. Evening after evening, since January the same year, the R.A.F. had been systematically attacking the German radar stations. It was impossible to draw any conclusions from these raids as to the part of the coast on which the invasion was planned; for wherever they were stationed—up at Ostend or down at Brest—all installations without exception kept receiving continual, and often very hot, visits from British bombers.

"Nothing of interest," the radar officer reported at naval staff headquarters in Paris.

The hands of the clock moved slowly toward midnight. For the past few days the staff of Gruppe West had held a short conference at eleven-thirty nightly. Something indefinable was in the air, something that could be felt and guessed, but which no one could put his finger on.

It was known at Gruppe West that a few weeks before the enemy had held a great invasion exercise off the south coast of England. It had taken place by moonlight at low tide and in the small hours, thus enabling certain conclusions to be drawn as to the intended moment of the invasion. Moonlight and tide, the hours of high and low water, must determine the moment, and it had accordingly been calculated that the landing would have to take place between June 2 and 7. The next days favorable for the Allies would not be until a few weeks later. But during the first days of June storms and heavy seas made an invasion most unlikely. Admiral Krancke, head of Gruppe West, employed the time to go on an inspection tour in the South of France. And even at the conference shortly before midnight on June 5 it was merely stated that that night again the invasion would probably be "off."

"The wind is already force five to six," the meteorologist informed the meeting. "It may still freshen up to seven. For this reason in my opinion there is no danger tonight."

"To judge by radar observation I entirely agree," the radar officer added. All stations had reported themselves in working order, even those which had been attacked by the R.A.F.

"The set on Cape La Hague on the Cherbourg peninsula reports echoes round the Isle of Wight, but . . ."

"Are there any signs that it is not an ordinary coastal convoy?" the Chief of Staff asked.

"No, sir, none at all."

Nor was there any other news of a change in the situation. Before midnight the lights went out in the large block of apartments near the Bois de Boulogne which housed the top German naval staff in France, only two officers remaining on night duty.

Exactly two hours later, at ten minutes to two, telephones rang at every bedside. The receivers were lifted sleepily. But what followed got everybody wide awake.

"Please come at once to the map room." It was the familiar voice of the Staff Officer Operations, Captain Wegener. "I think this is the invasion."

This acted like an electric shock. Never had the officers got into their clothes so fast. The Navy had always set great store by correct turnout, but now some of them ran to the map room practically as they were, even the Chief of Staff, Admiral Hoffmann, standing before the map in his dressing gown. The first hitch had already occurred. No telephone or teleprinter line was working between Paris and the Cherbourg peninsula—the Maquis had cut all the wires precisely at 1:45 A.M.

Preparations for this emergency had, however, been made, and radio links set up, through which—the only means of communication that remained intact—the first accurate reports were now coming in from individual radar installations, above all from those in the peninsula's neighborhood.

The reports were strange enough.

"Many echoes on the cathode-ray tube." Hesitantly the range and bearing of these echoes were given as if they were normal targets.

"Unusual interference on the set," the radar unit at Cape Harfleur reported. "A large number of echoes on the screen." And, after some time:

"We have shifted away from the enemy interference to another frequency, but the echoes are still there. A large number of echoes."

By now it was already known in Paris that the large number of echoes was not due to interference but indicated the Allied invasion fleet sailing toward the French coast. It was a fleet of a size hitherto unknown. There were so many ships that the technicians behind the radar sets thought naturally of large-scale interference. They were not inexperienced but they did not suspect such a mass of targets swarming on the water. Yet the truth was that the Allied invasion fleet was on its way.

"The invasion fleet is here, General."

The officer at the other end of the line did not believe his ears. What was this nonsense the Navy was talking? Tonight? Of course not. The English were not so stupid as to come on an unfavorable night. His answer was more than skeptical:

"Are you sure your radar isn't playing tricks on you? You're probably detecting sea gulls or something."

"Please regard the report as absolutely reliable."

By now it was two-thirty in the morning. The first hurried reports had been followed by more precise details. There was news of parachute landings; whole squadrons of gliders were reported from certain points on the Cherbourg peninsula. It was already clear that it was toward this last that the Allied shipping movement pointed. The radar units had recovered from their first shock and now reported faithfully everything their screens disclosed of the size and bearing of the enemy fleet. At the same time individual installations were coming under heavy bombardment by the R.A.F.

But at C.-in-C. West's and Hitler's headquarters no one wanted to believe in the invasion. Perhaps it was a diversion or a feint? The Army Groups on the coast were, indeed, brought to readiness; but before anyone decided on wider countermeasures, many precious hours of covering darkness were lost.

In the meantime Admiral Krancke, who was at that moment at Arcachon, was told of the situation by his Chief of Staff. After putting a few questions he ordered the signal: *Mass landing in the Seine estuary.*

This was the signal to start the Navy's anti-invasion measures.

A little later everything that the Navy still possessed on this coast—and that was little enough—left port to fall on the flank of the enemy armada, the greatest assembly of ships the world had ever seen.

"In this weather they won't launch an invasion," the commander of the old German torpedo boat *Moewe* opined, shaking his head. Yet at that very moment his senior watch-keeper appeared with a new radio signal. *Numerous enemy parachute and airborne troops landed near Caen.*

"An odd feeling, don't you think? For months we have been waiting for it to start, and now, when it's probably happening, it just seems incredible."

The *Moewe,* with two other torpedo boats, *T 28* and *Jaguar,* was advancing at high speed against "targets located in the Channel," as the phrase used in the order went which hustled them from their base in Le Havre. What kind of targets? To judge by the many radio messages which were humming through the air, some of which they could pick up themselves, the Allies must have put to sea with their whole invasion fleet. And yet it seemed like a dream to the men on the torpedo boats, perhaps for the simple reason that it was quite impossible to imagine how their three little ships could achieve anything against the entire British battle fleet, which without any doubt must have sailed as well.

"There, look at that."

The torpedo-boat unit was just overtaking a patrol flotilla which had sailed from Le Havre before them and was on the same course. The little boats were making heavy weather—the 18th Patrol Flotilla was made up of every possible type of craft flung together.

"That one looks like a Rhine tug," someone on the *Moewe's* bridge remarked.

"Good lord, it actually is a paddle steamer!"

"Vintage 1910, I should say. What price a river steamer against the British invasion fleet!" The speaker shook his head. But the laughter which followed had a liberating effect.

In the meantime dawn broke in the east. Soon the milky gray

of the first hours of morning was lying over the Seine estuary, and quickly it became lighter. Suddenly the torpedo officer of the *Moewe*, looking through his range-finder, made out some ghostly shapes ahead, scarcely visible on the western horizon, which was still dark. He wiped his eyes as if by this gesture he could drive the apparition away. But the apparition remained; there could be no doubt about it. Before them, less than 12 kilometers ahead, sailed a fleet of vast proportions which could only be that of the Allied invasion.

Range 100, the report was passed up from the range-finder. Everybody trembled in excited suspense. Only ten kilometers now—ten kilometers between the three German torpedo boats and the British battleships and cruisers. Five of them could already be made out clearly, guarded on the flanks by zigzagging destroyers. This whole force would itself be guarding the main body of the invasion fleet—the troopships and landing craft of all kinds moving toward the French coast. How could anyone get to the vital center of this armada? It seemed almost impossible, especially now, as the light improved from minute to minute.

Now the range-finder showed a range of 085; only eight and a half kilometers from the nearest target, which by now had been identified as the British battleship *Warspite*. Surely the German ships should have been discovered long ago. But as it was they still continued to sail on at high speed against the enemy.

Stander Z vor! It was the attack order for the torpedo boats.

At the same time, from *T 28*, the commander of the torpedo-boat flotilla signaled over the VHF.

Open fire!

This was against the fighter-bombers, which at last had taken notice of the Germans and were coming in to attack. They were met by a hail of shells.

"Why doesn't the big stuff ahead just blow us to bits?" wondered the gunnery officer aboard the *Moewe*.

"They can't fire for laughing," someone suggested ironically.

The 16- and 11-inch shells would rip the torpedo boats to

pieces at the first hit. But still the British did not fire, apparently completely unconcerned with a possible German torpedo attack. The only thing that now happened, after the failure of the fighter-bombers' attack, was that other aircraft tried to lay a smoke screen across the unit, intending to blind them. A few seconds later the patrol leader gave the order to prepare to fire torpedoes.

"Stand by to fire a spread salvo of six," called the torpedo petty officer.

"All set?" The commander called.

"All ready, sir. Please turn."

The torpedo tubes mounted on the starboard beam, the boats had to turn to port at full speed. Everything now depended on the torpedo officer, who had to fire in the fraction of a second when he had the enemy ship directly in his sights. A moment later the chance would be lost because the boat would have turned too far and the "tin fish" would run off course.

Just before the smoke screen blotted out the view the six torpedoes of the *Moewe* hissed out of their tubes, heading directly for the British battleship. It was the same with the other boats—18 torpedoes plowed forward in a wide spread toward the Allied invasion fleet. Would any strike home? It was impossible to observe anything from the German boats because at this moment a tornado of shelling broke over them. Their crews could neither hear nor see—the English had opened up with every gun they had. Ahead, straddling and astern of them, tall fountains rose from the sea, one kind colored red or orange, the other green or yellow—the colors being designed to indicate to the enemy gunnery control officers their own fall of shot.

Though every second could bring a decisive hit, the torpedo boats then started laying a smoke screen over the units of the 18th Patrol Flotilla, which were lying almost helpless under the heavy fire. Only then did the German ships begin to withdraw, zigzagging wildly. It was scarcely believable that they could escape from the forest of waterspouts, but nevertheless they did. At one moment the *Jaguar* seemed to have caught it.

A heavy shell beneath her bow threw up a mountain of water which fell back with terrific force over her fo'c'stle. But she merely shook herself a little and went on, zigzagging more wildly than ever to avoid the next hit.

This performance continued for almost half an hour, and, incredibly enough, not the smallest damage was caused. The proverbial luck which the torpedo boats had hitherto enjoyed on their missions in the Channel did not now forsake them. The sparks were flying from their funnels as they steamed back to harbor at 28 knots—the utmost speed of which their aged engines were capable.

One thing had become clear during this first attack on the invasion fleet: there was no way of getting near the heart of it, namely, the landing craft. Still, this might be possible at night, with E boats. These, too, were accordingly thrown in mercilessly, on an order from Gruppe West, representing the only action the Navy could take.

For months the Navy had accepted without question that the Allied landing would take place in the neighborhood of the Seine estuary, and all units which were still battleworthy were thus concentrated in this area. But what did they amount to? Five torpedo boats in Le Havre; 16 E boats in Cherbourg; seven more in Boulogne; and seven in Scheveningen and Ostend. At most one could add the four destroyers lying in the Gironde estuary and the three torpedo boats in Brest. But that was the whole of the German fighting force.

Official reports show the extent of the Allied opposition: 6 battleships, 2 monitors, 22 cruisers, 119 destroyers, 113 frigates and corvettes, 80 patrol boats, 360 M.T.B.'s and gunboats, and 25 mine-sweeping flotillas.

It was virtually suicide for the Germans to go out against this, and some commanders said so openly. But it was no good. *Attack with torpedoes at all costs,* went the new order; and so night after night the Germans sailed out to fire their torpedoes against the invasion fleet. Soon there was a visible shortage of torpedoes in Le Havre. The supply system no longer functioned efficiently. In Cherbourg there were torpedoes enough, but a break-through at night seemed utterly impossible, for the invasion fleet was guarded on both flanks by a dense barrier of battleships, cruisers, and destroyers. In spite of this the E boats managed to pierce this barrier and fire their torpedoes against the biggest troopships. But some of them found themselves encircled by enemy ships and lost their way back. "Shut your eyes and get through—anywhere . . ." was the maxim. When they opened their eyes they found that they had, in fact, broken right through the Allied fleet, so that they returned, not to their base in Cherbourg, but to Le Havre, which only aggravated the torpedo shortage.

But soon there was no longer need for torpedoes. An annihilating blow was shortly to hit the "phantom flotilla," as the BBC called the attackers of the British fleet.

Daring as their nightly raids were, their losses remained small, considering the storm of shells which the enemy now unleashed whenever they appeared. Two destroyers, one torpedo boat, and a number of E boats perished in this murderous struggle. Similarly, however, their successes were hardly noticeable amid the multitude of the enemy's shipping. Seeing that 4266 ships and landing craft sailed for the French coast on D-day, whatever the Germans managed to knock out was only a pinprick. During the first six days 64 Allied ships were sunk and 106 were hit and damaged.[1]

But this loss irritated the British High Command, and it was decided to put an end to the German phantom flotilla once and for all. On the evening of June 14, 1944, while the torpedo boats were preparing for a new night attack and while activity in the port of Le Havre was settling down for the night, the "alarm" sounded. Everything happened so quickly that the crews, hurrying to the shore shelters, were surprised by the first carpet of bombs. The sheds were hit, the quayside torn open; bombs fell into the water and on the boats; they punched craters

---

[1] This figure evidently includes air and mine casualties, not only those due to German *naval* actions. [Publishers' note.]

and threw masonry, dust, and heavy ironwork through the air. And this was only the first wave, the first squadron. When, at half-past two in the morning, the last aircraft had flown away, the work of destruction was complete.

Of the torpedo boats only *T 28* was undamaged, with the *Moewe* only just afloat; all the others had disappeared in the water. But even the *Moewe* was ablaze from stem to stern; she listed and pulled at her moorings till they snapped under the strain.

Only a handful of watchers standing on the wrecked jetty saw her last struggle as the *Moewe,* freed of her last fetters, eventually heeled over and quietly sank bow first.

It was half-past five in the morning, June 15, 1944. With a single stroke of their air force the Allies had destroyed everything that had so far opposed their invasion fleet. Now the whole burden of the German sea defense lay on the E boats (insofar as they had survived the murderous attack on Le Havre), the few U boats, and some "small battle units"—one-man torpedoes, explosive motorboats, and midget submarines.

12

"Negroes" and "Beavers"

Ｏｎ ａ ｍｏｏｎｌｉｔ ｎｉｇｈｔ ｅａｒｌｙ ｉｎ Ｊｕｌｙ, 1944, ｇｒｅａｔ
activity was to be observed on the beach west of Trouville,
which was usually so quiet. Narrow lanes had been cleared in
the beach defenses, and the men who were running busily up
and down were plainly not preparing for a *military* operation.
They were carefully lowering into the water long tubes which
looked like long, black Cuban cigars; there were always two of
these coupled together, one of them mounted a few inches above
the other.

Some of the men now got into the front parts of the upper
tubes; others bent down to talk to them and to make a few ad-
justments. Then came a last wave, a handshake—and a glass
dome was fixed over each man's head, looking like a round
dish cover. This was bolted down and made water- and airtight.

It was indeed a strange sight to see the "dish covers" floating
on the surface of the water. Set off against the smooth sea, they
glinted in the moonlight. Then they moved forward. No, they
were not just floating. They gathered speed and slowly disappeared into the night and the ocean. The course they set, how-

ever, was to take them within a few hours to the British invasion fleet.

This mysterious mechanism worked by a single man beneath his perspex dome was a torpedo—just that—with the difference that this familiar weapon was no longer being taken to the enemy ship by torpedo boat or U or E boat, but by a single man who would fire it only from a position close enough to the target to be sure of success. The Italians, the Japanese, and the English had used or tested such weapons successfully during the first years of the war. There were really two torpedoes. In the upper (or carrier) torpedo the pilot sat in the space which was normally given to the warhead. Slung below was the live torpedo, which he could release by a trigger and so fire. His aiming device consisted of a backsight—a notch in the glass just in front of his head—and a foresight in the form of an iron spike at the head of his carrier torpedo. With this he was supposed to aim accurately. There were other great difficulties. His tiny craft could do five knots at the most, if the batteries were not to be exhausted before he reached home. With even a moderate wind and sea he would be a plaything of the waves and unable to sail. Moreover, the nights chosen for operations had preferably to be light, since the one-man-torpedo pilot's head was only 18 inches above the waterline; his restricted vision would otherwise prevent him from locating the enemy.

Admiral Dönitz mentioned all these difficulties when reporting to Hitler on June 29, 1944. At that time the "negroes," as the Navy called them, were due shortly to begin operations on the invasion front.

"We shall be able to start operations with the first explosive motorboats soon as well," Dönitz said. "But all these weapons are naturally very dependent on the weather."

Hitler was obviously unperturbed by this reservation. His hopes were high. "Of course," he declared, "the enemy warships—particularly the battleships—must be attacked, just as the merchant ships are. Just imagine it: if England were to lose six to eight battleships in the Seine estuary, the strategical consequences would be enormous."

Dönitz looked at Hitler, aghast. Did he really believe you could sink *battleships* with one-man torpedoes? And six or eight of them! The Admiral hastened to stress his skepticism:

"Under present conditions the practical value of these small battle units has still to be proved. In any event, the air force is going to lay as many mines as possible in the Seine estuary. I believe that they are still the most effective weapon against the enemy supply system."

Hitler was not satisfied with this.

"We have *kept* laying mines in the Seine estuary," he pronounced. "The British, too, have kept laying mines in our supply routes. We follow them like a British bulldog following its master. Let us follow another of their examples. Let us concentrate all our forces against the invasion supply lines—send everything we have against them. It is incomparably more effective to sink a complete troopship than to fight against the troops and their weapons after they have disembarked. We forced the English out of Norway by cutting off their supplies with the air force, the U boats, and the battleships; now we must cut them off in the same way, with every weapon we have."

With these words Dönitz was dismissed. Norway, he thought, was in 1940. In those days the Navy was equal to the job. Then there was still a fleet and, even if the torpedoes were no good at the time, at least the U boats did not have to hide. Four years of war had passed since then. And now Hitler demanded the same effort from the Navy. What was worse, he seemed to think that the same results were possible. *With every weapon we have. . . .*

The single torpedo boat remaining in action against the invasion forces Dönitz now withdrew, for alone it was helpless against the enemy's numbers. The E boat flotillas had about 50 per cent of their strength left. A few U boats, equipped with "Snorkel," managed also to get close to the enemy supply ships, but only a minority came back undamaged.

With every weapon we have. . . . All that was left was the class of weapons classified collectively as "small battle units" —Lilliputian weapons, relying almost solely on the courage of those manning them. One-man torpedoes, explosive motor-boats, and midget submarines, "negroes," "martens," "lentils," "beavers," "newts," and "seals"—the Navy's last reserves.

The hours dragged by interminably for the pilot of the one-man torpedo. The motor humming monotonously as the double-cigar approached the Orne estuary (if it was on its course), the pilot strained his eyes to catch some sign of the enemy fleet.

Often pilots turned back after hours of dispiriting search. They no longer knew their position.

But now at long last he could make out an extended line of ships on the horizon—fast-moving ones which vanished again after a few minutes. Other ships, though, were almost stationary. The pilot's heart was in his throat. If he managed to keep calm, if he got his negro within range, his torpedo was bound to get home.

Was he close to the coast, perhaps off one of the Allies' mulberry harbors? Or had he met an enemy convoy out at sea? He could not know.

"Don't let them see me, don't let them spot me," he prayed.

He kept bearing toward the silhouettes, which kept coming nearer, growing bigger. As he watched through his little dome 18 inches or so above the water, they looked like great black monsters, though in reality they were only small warships, mine sweepers, and corvettes or, at most, destroyers. These only guarded the flanks of the landing ships. But there, *there* a bigger warship was coming within range of his torpedo—possibly a British cruiser, to judge from the outline. He was unable to judge speeds accurately, but she seemed to move more slowly than the others. The chance of scoring a hit was all the greater.

He pressed the trigger.

The connection with the warhead torpedo was broken and at the same time the torpedo was armed. Compressed air set it into motion and gave it a "kick," until, driven by its own electric motor, it disappeared in the direction of the warship. The lonely man beneath his glass dome waited. He did not know if he had guessed the distance accurately, whether the enemy would alter course, increase speed, or take some other evasive action during the one or two minutes the torpedo needed to run home. First a flash and then the thunder of an explosion jerked him from his thoughts. For seconds the cruiser stood out in a glow of red and yellow flames—then was enveloped in thick smoke. Only then did the negro pilot turn back and manage after many hours to find his own part of the coast and his comrades.

From this first attack only two of the one-man torpedoes failed to return. Most of them made no contact with the enemy, but those few who got near the invasion fleet were able to register hits. There was great rejoicing. The commander of the new units and the pilot who sank the British light cruiser of the *Aurora* class, an army clerk, were awarded the Knight's Cross. There were also many other decorations awarded. Perhaps, after all, this weapon could achieve something against the invasion fleet?

The next time the negroes went into action things were different. The English, who had not even considered the possibility of their existence during the first attack, were now keeping a close watch. The moment they saw something glinting in the moonlight on the calm sea they opened fire, for it could only be one of the glass domes. A few well-aimed shots with a light weapon were enough to eliminate this German "marvel," and in nearly every instance the pilot was mortally wounded. Some pilots were luckier. They fell asleep through strain or lack of oxygen under their tiny glass domes. The English soon lost their first terror of the "human torpedoes," and whenever they spotted one adrift they came alongside with their boats and picked up the negro with its exhausted pilot.

The losses of the German one-man torpedoes soon outran their few successes. From operations against the enemy 60 to 80 per cent of the negroes which had set out with such good wishes and high hopes failed to return. Some still reported "successes," but often their targets had only been wrecks lying off one of the invasion harbors, whose outlines rose high and ghostlike above the water at low tide. They included an old French battleship and other veteran warships, which the Allies had sunk at the beginning of the invasion to serve as breakwaters for artificial harbors. Time and again solitary negro pilots launched their torpedoes against these static, silent wrecks and believed that they had hit or sunk a battleship.

Meanwhile the losses mounted from operation to operation.

Did it make sense to send still more young men to their deaths? The glass dome was too treacherous; it glinted in the moonlight and was generally sighted by the enemy. If only one could dive with the negro; if only it could be developed into a midget U boat, which, once discovered, was not at the mercy of enemy guns on the surface. With such craft the idea of miniature naval warfare for coastal defense could be developed with some hope of success.

Kapitänleutnant Bartels had been thinking about midget submarines for a long time; more than that, he had actualy produced a blueprint of one. His name had been known to the Naval Staff since the spring of 1940, when as commander of the mine sweeper *M 1* he had been given the task, after the occupation of Norway, of building up coastal defense flotillas with local resources. He had accomplished this task with great skill and a wealth of practical imagination, and had gained a reputation for inventing and improvising. Thus, early in the war, he had worked on the idea of midget submarines, steered by one man, for coastal defense.

In 1942 Bartels wrote a memorandum in which he advanced the opinion that one day an adequate number of special weapons would be necessary to defend German-held coasts against an enemy assault. But such ideas were unpopular at a time when the Battle of the Atlantic seemed to be drawing to a close favorable to Germany.

Concerned lest he should be unable to push his midget-submarine idea far enough, if he submitted the memorandum through the normal channels, Bartels managed to smuggle his script into the brief case of the adjutant of Dönitz, who was then C.-in-C. U boats and inspecting the Atlantic coast. It seems certain that Dönitz read it, although at the time he had greater worries. The building program of normal, full-size U boats was about to be extended for attacks on Allied supply lines, and the development of the new types of U boat which were to be faster and more efficient under water was also to be pushed ahead. German industrial capacity was simply insufficient to produce new weapons which might not be used for some years.

When the Navy, in the autumn of 1943, created the small battle units, the situation had changed fundamentally. Now, in great haste, weapons were to be constructed, tested, and mass-produced which might stop the Allies' threatened assault on the continent of Europe.

Bartels, now promoted Korvettenkapitän, took a leading part in this. The first German midget submarine or "beaver" was built to his specification at the Flender shipyard in Lübeck. The U boat men affectionately called it *Adam*. But *Adam* gave trouble. At its first trial, in full view of OKM observers, it failed and sank. The prospects were not good.

Work went on, nevertheless, indefatigably. The invasion was approaching, and not a single "beaver" was ready to start. Only the negroes arrived in the Seine estuary—four whole weeks after the invasion had begun—and they were not very successful either. At about this time the first volunteers turned up at a small wood, surrounded by barbed wire, somewhere in the solitude of the Bay of Lübeck, a signaler rubbing shoulders with a petty officer, an infantryman with a pilot officer of the Luftwaffe. There were so many volunteers from all the services that only a proportion had been selected to come to this wood, the "Blaukoppel," to see their new beaver for the first time.

Training started at once. The small battle units' commander, Vice-Admiral Heye, left no doubt that fighting with the miniature weapons would be tough. His motto was: "I need *men!*"

Time was running short. In mid-August, when the Allies had

already broken out of the bridgehead, the first 20 training beavers were ordered to the Channel coast to attack the enemy supply lines while there was still a chance. With great difficulty they reached Fécamp, between Boulogne and Le Havre. Le Havre itself was already unusable. On the evening of August 29, 18 beavers put to sea. But the approach run to the lifelines of the enemy supply system was too long, and a sea and wind of force 4 to 5 created difficulties for the minute craft. They only succeeded in sinking two transports, one of which was a Liberty ship of 8000 tons. After that, the beavers could no longer remain even at Fécamp, and the general disorganization of the German resistance in France led to their withdrawal. But, in spite of this, new beavers continued to arrive at the "Blaukoppel," and still more volunteers were trained in them.

On an unfriendly November day in 1944 a number of heavy trucks drove down the roads of Holland toward the coast. They were towing odd-looking trailers, completely covered with tarpaulins.

"Halt! Army patrol."

It was a lieutenant wanting to check their movement orders. His men glanced inquisitively at the mysterious trailers.

"So you're going to Rotterdam? That's fine. I've got a lot of civilians and troops in the village who want to go there. We don't often get trucks with so much room to spare round this way. What have you got under the tarpaulins?"

"I'm afraid I can't tell you, sir. And I can't take anybody."

"Why not? You can take hundreds of people. Seven trucks and seven trailers! Just you see how many people can go under the tarpaulins alone."

The C.P.O. in charge of the column had been ordered to take his loads to Rotterdam in strictest secrecy and was becoming uneasy.

"May I talk to you for a minute in private, sir?"

A few minutes later he was able to drive on—without passengers. He had only had to let fall the word "secret," which was an accurate enough description of his load. The soldiers on the road gazed after the column in wonder till it was lost to view.

"They probably think we are taking the latest V-weapon for a ride," said one of the naval drivers with a grin.

As a matter of fact, the mysterious packaging on each of the trailers contained a beaver. Two flotillas, comprising 60 one-man submarines, were on their way to Rotterdam by different routes. From there they were to attack the Allied supply lines which stretched almost unhindered from England to the Scheldt and Antwerp. But before that there was a special mission for some of the boats on the Waal.

At Nijmegen a pair of important bridges spanned the river. During the German advance in 1940 our parachutists had taken these crossings by surprise and stopped the Dutch from blowing them up. Now, in 1944, the situation was reversed. The Americans had taken the bridge by surprise and were guarding it so well that the Luftwaffe was powerless to bomb it. Accordingly the Navy was called in. Despite a strict watch, frogmen succeeded in coming close and blowing up the railway bridge. But it was impossible to do the same with the equally important road bridge. The Allies had doubled their security precautions, and four heavy antisubmarine nets secured the river above the bridge, from which direction German attacks were possible, as the German front line was only about three miles away, on the east bank of the Waal.

The beavers were ordered to attempt everything in their power to blow up the bridge. After consulting air photographs, it was plain that the nets would have to be disposed of before one could get anywhere near the bridge itself. This meant there was no alternative to blowing up the nets first.

A search for suitable explosives disclosed 240 aerial land mines, which were converted and given a special filling with a specific gravity only a little greater than that of water. On X-day 60 of these at a time were lowered into the river at half-hour intervals a few miles above the nets. Slowly they sank to the river bed and there skipped on, pushed by the current, with comical little jumps. The speed of the current had been exactly calculated, and it was thus known when the majority of the first batch of 60 must hit the first net. For testing their time fuses five minutes were added to the time they should take to travel.

When a chain of explosions tore the first net to shreds, already the 60 mines destined for the second net were rolling and bowling along. Then a third group, and finally the last. In addition, a number of beavers had crept downriver to fire their torpedoes against the nets. As the enemy were all along the west bank, and a few miles above the bridge on *both* banks, and as they had orders to watch the river like hawks, this was anything but easy. The Americans fired at anything that floated, even if it was only a box or a dead cat. Since they could not lower them, the beaver pilots had camouflaged their periscopes with bundles of grass and weeds so that they appeared so many clumps peacefully floating down the river.

When they had fired their torpedoes the beavers turned back. Now their main task began, for all this had served only to destroy the nets. While the mine explosions thundered in the distance, the beavers took heavy tree trunks in tow and started again on their dangerous passage downstream. Slung beneath the tree trunks and additionally supported by buoyancy chambers were three-ton explosive charges. It was impossible just to let them drift, because the Waal made a wide bend before the bridge and the tree trunks would be driven against the bank.

For this reason the beavers towed the trunks and their enormous explosive charges to the end of the bend and there released them. Here, where they could see the bridge through their periscopes only 1000 yards away, the first net had hung only half an hour ago.

While the boats crept back, the trunks glided unhindered down the river. Concealed on top of them they carried a photoelectric cell. This was connected with a firing circuit which operated the moment a shadow fell on the cell from above . . . the shadow of the bridge.

Would it work? Were 240 mines enough to rip away the nets? Would one of the tree trunks really drift right under the bridge? If so, the bridge would be blown sky-high without fail.

German observers, from a high point behind the front lines, followed all this with mounting excitement. For some time now, hell had been let loose in the last three-quarter-mile stretch above the bridge. The mine explosions were masked by the mad firing of the enemy. For, after the disappearance of the first two nets, the Americans had naturally realized what was afoot and were raking the river with every kind of weapon to blow up floating explosives or anything else the Germans might have devised. This inferno was now continually punctuated by heavy detonations which could only come from the tree trunks blowing up with their loads.

But all this was above the bridge, perhaps 50 yards from the target. The party went on till dusk, and then the Germans turned away, disappointed. The bridge was still intact.

The next day air photographs yielded the explanation. Three net barrages had been destroyed. But the fourth and last had held, and caught up everything which had been designed to destroy the bridge.

From Rotterdam, the beavers were to operate on the enemy's supply lanes. Twenty times at least during these weeks, the last of 1944, they made sorties from their concrete pens and shelters.

"On the job tonight. The beavers are going into action."

Harbor tugs hove alongside to take the midget U boats in tow, like nothing so much as fat mother hens fussing over their chicks. The beavers were only 8.70 meters long and 1.45 meters in the beam and except for the small conning tower were submerged below the surface of the water when the pilot climbed into his cramped seat.

When the boats at last reached Hellevoetsluis, a lock north of the island of Goeree, the technical staff went over them once more with minutest care to make sure that these 30 or 40 of the Navy's tiniest craft were equipped for an operational run. They would have barely an hour before the lock gates were opened at high tide to let the pack through. Then out they would go into the darkness with their Opel engines stinking of gasoline, for the most part young volunteers of all ranks, setting out with brave hopes down the Maas toward the sea.

Yet how heavy the odds against them were! Only nights faintly illumined by the thin sickle of a new moon, when the sky was overcast and visibility poor, gave them a reasonable chance of not being spotted by enemy observers. Only in a calm sea and with a moderate wind, moreover, was the trip at all possible. Left to his own devices, the pilot squatted in his narrow seat. A few months' training had to suffice to teach him at least the rudiments of navigation. When he was able to run on the surface he was perhaps three feet above the level of the sea. That was too little for him to manage to see very far. How was he to find his bearings, after running for hours, to know where he was? A wrist compass, a little chart with his course marked on it, and a few instructions jotted on a scrap of paper were all the help he had.

His course had been previously charted for him by experienced navigators. Carrying two torpedoes, the beaver could do only four knots. The speed of the current near the Dutch coast averaged about the same, flying upstream at flood tide and seaward on the ebb. A midget U boat that tried to make headway against this current would make no progress and, sooner or later, would be lost. Time of starting and course had to be calculated so that the beaver could go out on the ebb tide and return home on the flood.

Yet the distances were not usually so short. This meant, therefore, that the boats had to wait for two, three, or even four tides.

"You start at exactly 0700 hours, course 260 degrees," the navigating officer ashore instructed the pilot. He impressed upon him what alterations of course he would have to make at what time to reach, first, the West Scheldt, and then, passing the outlying islands and Flushing, enter the Scheldt proper. All these instructions were based on the hypothesis that the speed of the boat and the strength of the current were known factors, that the start was made on the dot, and that the navigational gear of the craft was capable of keeping her exactly on the plotted course.

But what if something went wrong? If the pilot had any trouble, if something took him off his course or forced him to dive? There were dozens of possibilities of this happening. He might be spotted and caught unawares by enemy observers, especially aircraft; adverse winds might suddenly spring up; he might be swept out of his course by unforeseen currents from ahead or abeam; he might run aground on a sandbank, in which case the beaver would inevitably remain on the mud till the next flood tide; or a host of other mishaps might occur.

The midget U boats that succeeded, however, in getting as far as the Scheldt were almost certain to run up against the enemy, for one of the Allies' most vital lines of communication from England to the front in Germany passed up the Scheldt to Antwerp. Here there was an almost constant stream of shipping, closely covered on both sides by escort vessels and protected by ships of war.

"Like the traffic in the Königsallee in Düsseldorf," said the beaver men who watched from afar the spectacle of this nightly, and generally illuminated, procession from the southern tip of the island of Schouwen, which was still in German hands.

Only when the beavers arrived was there an interval in this procession of ships. The English, needless to say, were able as well as the Germans to calculate when all the favorable conditions necessary for the operations of a one-man U boat were present on the same day. Besides, they could tell from the local reports of their aircraft if the beavers were on the warpath.

SM—SM—SM . . . . Their radio flashed the warning every second, with a position given—and the flow of supply ships dried up. Often the beavers were successful in holding up supplies to Antwerp by their mere appearance for several days. Of course the enemy's propaganda did all it could to make this midget arm ridiculous. And yet they feared it, well aware that

28, 30, or 40 beavers operating together in a relatively small area represented a serious danger.

While the stream of shipping dried up, the pack of destroyers, trawlers, corvettes, and frigates was unleashed. In addition, hundreds of special aircraft joined in the hunt.

Nevertheless, betweeen December, 1944, and April, 1945, the beavers sent to the bottom some 90,000 tons of enemy shipping in the Scheldt. One individual pilot, Senior Midshipman Langsdorff, succeeded in slipping into the harbor of Antwerp and firing both his torpedoes into the lock gates so that the docks were put out of action for some 20 days. But he never returned. The majority of the beaver pilots never got back, sooner or later falling a prey to Allied air or naval forces. Our losses totaled 60 to 70 per cent, only a few of our pilots escaping with their lives from their crippled or sinking craft.

Take Able Seaman Engelage. Not far from the Hook of Holland he was suddenly attacked by a British fighter-bomber. One of the first bursts of fire from the aircraft's gun smashed the stern of his beaver to smithereens and destroyed the diving gear. The midget U boat capsized and sank.

Everything happened in a flash. Engelage could not climb out. As the boat rapidly settled deeper in the water he actually experienced a second of elation that he had escaped the hail of enemy bullets unscathed. But how did that help him now, when he was on the brink of death by drowning? Spellbound, he gaped at the water gushing up into his seat from his damaged boat. It completely soaked him and was rapidly rising higher.

Faster, faster! Speed was the only possible salvation. The beaver must become entirely filled with water, for only so could the outside pressure of the sea be counteracted and he opened the little conning-tower hatch to clamber out.

But how far is he already submerged? Second by second, the pressure of the water increased as he sank foot by foot deeper into the waves. Could he still stand the pressure? Wouldn't it burst his lungs?

Mechanically Engelage went through the drill he had practiced a thousand times. Mechanically he slipped the safety jacket over his head and groped with his free hand for the stopcock of the compressed-air cylinder.

Fresh hope surged through him. The water here couldn't be so very deep. He was within a stone's throw of the shore. Say not more than 30 or at most 60 feet deep. Now, as he sat here in the water, he grabbed at the release of the conning-tower hatch and was actually able to push the door open. Frantically he opened the valve of the compressed-air cylinder and the air hissed out into the rubber dinghy attachment. Now he was climbing onto his seat. With his last remnant of strength he wriggled out of the conning tower and felt himself carried upward by his safety jacket and, above all, by the tightly inflated dinghy to which he was clinging.

Yes, he was rising, shooting upward! The pressure eased, his head was free, he could breathe again. His first sensation was a wild joy; he had made it—escaped his watery grave.

The whole business had not lasted 30 seconds. The British fighter-bomber is still there, the pilot circling just above the surface of the sea. For the duration of one heartbeat Engelage stared upward, terrified, dreading the worst. But there was the Englishman touching his fingers to his forehead in salute! The German grinned back and feebly waved his free hand. The Englishman hovered around until he saw his enemy haul himself into his rubber dinghy and then with another flourish of his hand flew off toward the west.

Twice during these months the beavers suffered heavy blows that were not the doing of the enemy. The first was in January, 1945.

Once again the conditions for a start were favorable. The boats were lying at Hellevoetsluis, the "ground staff" making their final checkup, the pilots being briefed. Suddenly loud warning shouts were heard outside the room in which the last instructions were being given. Some of the men were on their way to the door when a violent explosion shattered the little harbor basin behind the lock. The house threatened to cave in, plaster from the ceiling raining onto the heads of the beaver pilots.

"Air raid!" someone yelled.

The men tumbled out through the doors and windows to seek safety in the open. In a matter of seconds another detonation followed. There was a wild commotion in the little harbor basin. A houseboat moored in front of the lock had apparently been hit—timber was flying through the air. A flood wave a yard high tossed the midget U boats about like shuttlecocks, flinging them against the harbor wall. Most of them disappeared under water, and altogether the casualties and damage were considerable.

"But the aircraft—where were the aircraft?" It was also remarkable that the A.A. guns had not fired a shot. Finally it turned out there had been no air raid. One of those who had been outside by the boats enlightened his comrades:

"Some idiot must have mistaken the compressed-air valve which fires the torpedoes for something else. It suddenly started hissing and before we could raise a finger the torpedo shot out like greased lightning and began careening madly about—first it struck the wall over there, then it turned and headed for the lock, bounced off again, and exploded there on the bank."

Everyone looked. A black gap yawned where only a few minutes ago the towpath ran.

"Lucky it didn't go off when it hit the lock gates!"

The arming mechanism had not run out soon enough for that. That was why the torpedo first ricocheted a couple of times before exploding.

"And the second explosion?"

"The flood wave smashed all the boats into one another. Then another torpedo got loose and hit the houseboat over there."

The result of the catastrophe was that only four or five beavers were still afloat—a flotilla of nearly 30 boats destroyed at one blow. A larger vessel had been flung half onto the pier. Dead and wounded lay buried everywhere under the debris.

From then on the beaver pilots gave Hellevoetsluis a wide

berth, preferring to risk the longer route via the Hook of Holland, while the boats were made ready for operations at Rotterdam. But there, too, on March 6, 1945, the same misfortune took place as two months previously behind the canal lock.

This time the consequences were even more devastating, as most of the pilots had already gone on board when the torpedo went off. Hardly anyone escaped the fury of the explosion except those who had already left the harbor. For the second time the midget U boat men were "hoist with their own petard."

A similar though less disastrous accident happened in these weeks to a midget U boat of the "seal" type in the open sea.

The seals were an improvement on the beavers. Rather bigger and manned by a crew of two—a captain and an engineer—they were, however, only ready for operational use in the last months of the war. Whereas the beaver had a displacement of only six and a quarter tons, that of the seal with its load of torpedoes was as much as 15 tons. The midget formations of the German Navy had altogether 324 beavers, 390 newts (another one-man U boat type), and 250 seals. The last-named operated against the enemy from Ymuiden in Holland.

On one such operation a British destroyer crossed the bows of a seal. Evidently the British had not yet detected the presence of the U boat. This was a heaven-sent chance to attack, and at the right moment the German pressed the release firing push of his torpedo.

The boat quivered from stem to stern. The jar was more violent than usual after firing. The two men on board the seal were suddenly pressed against the back of their seats. The slow-moving boat shot forward at trebled speed.

It was as if a giant fish had seized hold of the seal and were tearing it along. With horror the men perceived that they could not keep their depth. However hard they pulled on the diving rudder the boat was wrenched to the surface—unless something happened it would surface in sight of the destroyer.

The engineer quickly lighted on the explanation and reported to the captain,

"The port torpedo's still in the rack—it's jammed!"

Indeed, the jammed torpedo was pulling the whole boat forward by the propulsive force of its own fast-running electrical machinery, so that they were heading straight for the British destroyer. Through his periscope the captain descried the enemy warship racing toward him at an uncanny speed. Meanwhile the fuse of the torpedo had become primed. If it actually hit the destroyer the seal would be blown to kingdom-come together with its victim.

The periscope was now well above the surface, even the tiny conning tower cutting through the waves. As the craft rushed toward its target its bows were churning up a wave of foam that could be seen a mile away.

Only 150 yards separated them now from the destroyer. On board, the British had become alive to the danger and were opening fire with machine guns and revolvers on the monstrous thing frenziedly rushing toward them. If it maintained its headlong course it would strike the vessel exactly on the stern.

Meanwhile the Germans in the seal had put their helm to starboard with all their might. Even if the effect was hardly perceptible, it did influence the course of the crazy craft. As the destroyer also altered course at full speed in the nick of time the seal just whizzed past its stern. She passed so close that the sailors on board the destroyer could actually pepper the "sea monster," now recognized as a midget submarine, with hand grenades. The U boat disappeared again into the wastes of the sea as suddenly as she surfaced.

Yet, as it happened, in this way both ships were saved without harm to their crews.

It was the seals which, for the first exercise of their new and still-green crews, made the so-called "butter trips" to Dunkirk. In place of torpedoes large canisters of foodstuffs were clamped to the hull of the boat. These tiny provision ships sailed from Ymuiden, dived below the sharply watched enemy supply lanes, and, often after days, made delivery in the silted-up harbor of Dunkirk in order to bring a mite of help to the starving garrison.

13

The *Tirpitz*

FOR THE MEN ON BOARD THE TIRPITZ THE NIGHT OF September 22, 1943, had passed without any special incident. Many watches and little sleep, as had been the routine ever since their ship, representing the principal threat to the Allied convoys to Russia, had been lying in Norwegian waters. Men who had just been relieved at the end of their watch stood ready for muster on the upper deck.

Suddenly shouts rang across from the bows of the ship:

"A periscope! A periscope!"

Simultaneously there was a crack of rifle fire—anchor sentries in the forecastle were firing down into the water close to the side. In a twinkling the battleship which had been peacefully dozing in its morning slumber was transformed into an ants' nest, as loud-speakers droned incessantly through the decks: *Close watertight doors—U boat alarm—Close watertight doors —U boat alarm. . . . Close watertight doors. . . .*

The next moment a midget submarine surfaced close to the hull of the *Tirpitz.* Before further fire could be opened on the vessel the partly glazed upper deck was lifted and two Englishmen climbed out of their seats, raising their hands above their heads in token of surrender. A launch brought them to the gangway as the submarine, which the Germans had meanwhile taken in tow, sank to the bottom under the eyes of the staring sailors—its crew had taken the precaution of opening the flooding valves.

On the upper deck of the battleship the officer of the watch made haste toward his prisoners, the strain of whose exploit was written on both their faces. Yet they saluted the German officer correctly.

Hurriedly he asked a few questions, but the Englishmen did not reply. This was not the moment for a long interrogation. The *Tirpitz* was standing by—other submarines might be lurking ready to attack. The Germans erroneously assumed that the enemy had intended to fire torpedoes at the battleship. Had any more submarines got through the net barrage? How did they manage to get inside the solid, triple screen? There was only one possible explanation: they must have picked the moment at daybreak when the supply steamer was let into the netted cage. The barrage had to be opened for just a few minutes then and the Englishmen must have taken advantage of those minutes to slip through unobserved.

Still, there was no time now for such speculations. Another such dangerous assailant might surface at any moment.

And, in fact, as the machine guns opened up defensively from the decks, at about 150 yards from the *Tirpitz* another Lilliputian submarine surfaced. The very first bursts of fire so riddled it that it slid below the surface. Two British sailors came up in their lifebelts and swam to a buoy, from which they were later picked up.

The hellish concert continued. On board the *Tirpitz* they had spotted yet a third midget submarine, still outside the net barrage. Suddenly it shot out of the water like a tuna fish trying to leap the net, but was instantly deluged with a hail of bullets and similarly sank.

Meanwhile the two Englishmen were standing amidships on the lower deck under guard of one of the *Tirpitz's* crew. They were both very nervous. The sentry was struck by the way that one of them kept stealing a glance at his wrist watch, but before he had time to decide whether he ought to report this, the following happened:

The group was standing on the port side. Another quick glance at the wrist watch, this time quite significantly, and the two Englishmen strode quickly to the starboard side of the ship, the sentry following. At the very same instant the *Tirpitz* was seized by a powerful force and lifted perceptibly up, to the thud of a heavy explosion below water. With a splash the mighty hull of the battleship fell back and rocked itself to a standstill.

So they had got away with it after all. The two Englishmen who had succeeded in slipping through the net cage had attached a heavy limpet mine to the battleship's keel. An attempt to attach another one under the bows failed because they were forced to surface owing to the breakdown of their diving apparatus. The ship only suffered a trifling leak, but the shock of the explosion lifted the turbines out of their bearings, rendering the engines useless for several months. The British Admiralty breathed more freely—the *Tirpitz* had long been a thorn in its flesh.

This mighty sister ship of the *Bismarck*, sunk in 1941, with her eight 15-inch, twelve 5.9-inch, eighteen 4.1-inch, and sixteen 3.7-cm. guns, represented the most serious menace to the vital Allied sea route to the U.S.S.R. Her 138,000-horsepower engines gave the *Tirpitz* a maximum speed of 31 knots, and she carried four to six Arado aircraft on board. The crew of 2500 men were divided into 12 divisions. Fully loaded and fully equipped with fuel and ammunition, the ship had a displacement of 42,000 tons. The British had more than once experienced the concentrated power of this giant when their aircraft came in to attack her and the *Tirpitz* spat fire from all her guns.

At the time the crew of the *Tirpitz* had not been able to understand why, in May, 1941, "big brother" *Bismarck* had been allowed to break out into the Atlantic all alone. When, chased by the whole British fleet, the *Bismarck* finally succumbed, the news was a specially heavy blow to the men of the *Tirpitz.*

"Why weren't we sent out with her?" they wondered. "If we had been there this would never have happened."

The two ships had trained together in the Baltic; they had often taken each other in tow. However, the Naval Command had decided that the *Tirpitz,* which first became operational at the end of February, 1941, was not ready two months later to be sent into action along with the *Bismarck.* Nearly a year later, on January 14, 1942, the *Tirpitz,* the only surviving heavy German battleship, was sent to Norway.

On March 6, 1942, the *Tirpitz* came out for the first time to attack a convoy bound for Murmansk. But the weather was bad with low visibility, and although she cruised around for two days betweeen Jan Mayen Island and Bear Island she failed to find the convoy, only one straggler being sunk by an escorting destroyer. But the British also, who were after her with a battleship squadron, failed to locate the *Tirpitz.* Not until March 9, west of the Lofotens, did the German battleship receive a visit from British torpedo-carrying aircraft.

It was icy cold on board, the keen, driving wind cutting through even the thick leather overalls of the sailors manning the guns.

Suddenly a lookout reported from the foretop:

"Aircraft bearing 210 degrees."

All the flak crews on the ship sprang to action. The experts at identifying aircraft were searching the sky with their glasses. Shortly they picked up the enemy rapidly drawing nearer, counting seven—14—21 dots in the sky. The next thing they made out was that the dots were single-engined biplanes with undercarriage; they had therefore taken off from an aircraft carrier.

"Twenty-one Swordfish and Albacores!" the reports flashed to the flak control station. "Torpedo aircraft with fighter escort."

"Follow director!"

Like wickedly buzzing bumblebees the Tommies came in to the attack. Astern of the ship they divided in order to catch the *Tirpitz* in a two-pronged assault, flying in simultaneously from port and starboard. Suddenly the thunder crashed from the 5.9-inch twin turrets and the 4.1-inch flak. Yellow tongues of flame spat from the long barrels. The sharp barking of the latter together with the dry growl of the 5.9's alone made a fiendish racket until the enemy were close enough for the 3.7-cm. flak to add their yapping to the chorus.

Shellbursts appeared just below the aircraft. With the second salvo a direct hit blew the first machine to pieces. The others rocked and danced as if in a heavy gale. Immediately the group broke formation, and now, diving recklessly close to the surface of the sea, the pilots tried singly to drop their torpedoes as near as possible to the ship.

In no time at all the range was down to less than 2000 yards, and now the four-barreled pom-poms and light flak were rattling away, hurling a wall of fire at the racing aircraft as they skimmed the sea. The flash could be seen distinctly every time an aircraft was hit. One after another they hurtled blazing into the water. And yet the British kept on, still dropping their torpedoes into the inferno.

The *Tirpitz* had become a volcano spewing fire in all directions.

A Swordfish raced toward the ship, ablaze, but still flying stubbornly on, stubbornly straight ahead. From a distance of 200 yards its torpedo splashed into the sea. As the aircraft climbed away, it flew once again into a solid cone of 2-cm. pom-pom fire and crashed into the waves in a cloud of spume. But its torpedo was speeding toward the ship.

"Torpedo course 290 degrees! Torpedo course 110 degrees! Torpedo course 240 degrees!"

The lookouts chanted in a babel of confusion. Six torpedo courses were reported almost simultaneously and all of them different. At full speed—31 knots—the *Tirpitz* twisted and turned. The captain ordered a dozen alterations of course to avoid the torpedoes. The helm went hard over from one side to the other, and all this at full speed. The chief engineer doubted whether his steering gear could stand this excessive strain.

"It must!" the captain called back.

Only the four twin turrets of the ship's main armament were silent; the 15-inch guns took no part in the battle. But everything else was now blazing away at the maximum rate of fire, so that the light gray paint at the mouths of the gun barrels blistered and scorched to a brown-black mass. The men serving the 2-cm. pom-poms stood ankle deep in cartridge cases. If anyone found a second in which to glance aft at the wake of the ship he could see that the *Tirpitz*, though traveling at full speed, was spinning as if on a turntable.

Still the British refused to break off the action, for all that their little group was melting away. More than half their aircraft were destroyed, had crashed blazing into the sea with black plumes of rising smoke, or disintegrated in the air.

After 11 minutes the battle was over as suddenly as it began. Unbelievingly, the German sailors gaped at one another. Every minute they had expected the ship to stagger as she was hit, yet nothing had happened. More than 20 torpedoes had been counted, but all had missed their mark or had been avoided in time.

With a sigh of relief the captain looked at the grinning faces of the two officers on the bridge who had been transmitting his orders and for 11 minutes shouting the torpedoes' courses into his ears.

"Well, God must have kept His fingers crossed," he remarked. Next, he turned to the reports of aircraft shot down. According to them the enemy had lost about 15 machines, though it had been impossible to fix the exact number in the headlong rush and confusion. The German destroyer squadron reported three shot down besides one of the *Tirpitz's* own Arados which had been brought down by a British Albacore.

According to a British radio message, only three aircraft returned to their carrier.

Nevertheless, another attacking formation—this time Skuas
—was already on its way to give the *coup de grâce* to the battleship which the British Admiralty believed to be very seriously
damaged. But when a few hours later these aircraft appeared on
the scene of the battle the *Tirpitz* had vanished without a trace.
Even their wide, searching sweeps produced no result—the battleship had long since steamed out of the battle area at 28
knots and disappeared in the direction of Narvik into the West
Fjord.

A few hours later, however, the first agents' reports from Norway reached London:

*The Tirpitz lies at her moorings in the Alta Fjord. No damage
can be ascertained.*

As always after such a frustrated enterprise, the British now
left no stone unturned to put an end to the *Tirpitz*. Their un-
easiness at the unaffected strength of the German battleship
was increased when, in September, 1943, escorted by the battle
cruiser *Scharnhorst* and ten German destroyers she made a successful raid on Allied installations at Spitsbergen. The British
Admiralty anxiously demanded what progress had been made
with the training of midget-submarine personnel. Twelve days
after the Spitsbergen operation there ensued the exciting incident, already described, of the midget submarines inside the net
barrage protecting the *Tirpitz*.

It took six months to repair the serious damage to the battleship's engines. Apparently the British were well informed of
this, for hardly was she ready to put to sea again when, on April
3, 1944, several dozen Martlet aircraft surprisingly appeared
over the mountains along the fjord and swooped down on the
battleship like a swarm of hornets. Many German sailors were
still running to man their guns when they were hit by the air-
crafts' furiously blazing guns. Zooming at 90 or at most 120 feet
above the upper deck, the Martlets dropped their bombs and
scored 15 hits. Again the attack lasted 11 whole minutes.

One aircraft crashed onto the second 5.9-inch turret to starboard. It was not a Britisher, but a ship-borne aircraft of our own. A direct hit on deck had torn it away from the catapult and hurled it into the air. The deck occupied by the starboard watch of lookouts, who had just been awakened by the alarm bell, also received direct hits. The losses were terrible; 168 dead and 320 wounded lay about the shattered decks. Yet when the British appeared shortly afterward with bombers to finish off the *Tirpitz,* which was now drifting in the fjord, they were still met by furious and effective fire from her flak.

The Luftwaffe had not succeeded in spotting the British squadron in time, which was the reason why not a single German fighter appeared on the scene. It was very difficult to get the Luftwaffe Command to fulfill the demands of the Navy for reconnaissance and protection. The main reason for this state of affairs was that the increasingly heavy air attacks on the home country were taxing the Luftwaffe to the utmost; it is relevant, too, that Göring never had much use for the Navy.

The repairs to the *Tirpitz* were again carried out in Norway. Repeated air attacks in July and August, 1944, being unsuccessful, the British decided to bring up heavy land-based bombers. The machines started from Scotland and landed after the attack on a Russian airfield at Archangel. The first attack of this kind with 15 heavy bombers took place on September 15, 1944; a direct hit was gained, and several bombs hit the water at deck level of the *Tirpitz.* The forward top deck was destroyed with all the anchor gear. Once again not a single German fighter was there.

The damage this time was so heavy that it was practically impossible to carry out repairs in Norway. It was imperative to take the ship to the west if she was not to fall into the hands of the enemy. At that time the German front was being drawn back from the north of Finland and Norway to new positions west of the Lyngs Fjord. The *Tirpitz* limped painfully into the Sandesund, west of Tromsö. For the time being, she was to remain there as a floating battery.

This last attack took place on October 19, 1944. Another heavy attack from the air inflicted further damage on October 29. And then came November 12, 1944.

At last the most successful group of German fighters, the 5th Fighter Squadron, had been detailed to protect the *Tirpitz*. Its leader, Major Ehrler, and one of the pilots, Lieutenant Schuck, had shot down 200 enemy aircraft up to date. They had all been fighting during the last weeks of the embittered struggle in North Finland, during which there had been no failures in either personnel or material. Now, however, communications with the base on the new airfield at Bardufoss were not functioning properly. It was under these not exactly pleasing conditions that the eight pilots detailed to protect the German battleship were waiting to go into action on November 12.

A report came through that a squadron of British bombers was flying across the sea. It was subsequently added that the British were flying to Sweden and shaping their course toward the *Tirpitz* across neutral territory.

"They're flying through Sweden in comfort as far as the Tromsö Fjord, and we're not even allowed to attack them."

Six pilots were already sitting at the controls of their machines. The other two remained listening to the reports of the course taken by the British bomber squadron until the last moment.

Then the alarm was given, and red rockets soared skyward. Everything was functioning without a hitch. Feldwebel [1] Müller was flying aircraft "Y"—the one that remained in constant communication with the base. The German fighters were making straight for the battleship's berth. The map showed a little valley to the south of it, and it was there they intended to attack the enemy.

Three minutes' flight must bring them there; the British should arrive ten minutes later, provided they kept to the course they had taken. At that moment Müller heard something which

---

[1] British equivalent Flight Sergeant.

made him doubt the evidence of his own ears. But he had heard correctly: the radio operator at Bardufoss repeated the message agitatedly several times over:

All cyclists assemble over garden fence!

The "cyclists" were the Messerschmitt fighters, the "garden fence" meant the airfield. Now, when they had arrived at the scene of action, were they being ordered back to the base?

Full! Full! Full! the wireless operator's voice was saying now. That meant with all available speed. What was happening in Bardufoss? Could it be that the British were not attacking the *Tirpitz*, but the airfield instead?

The squadron leader arrived at that conclusion at the same moment. The British squadron had suddenly turned off from its original course, veering westward toward Bardufoss. Nobody noticed that not more than half the bombers were involved in the feigned attack, the other half—29 aircraft—continuing to fly straight toward the *Tirpitz*. The British maneuver was thus crowned with success, for the German battleship remained without fighter protection, as all fighters were hastening back with the utmost speed they could muster to protect the airfield.

It was not until the British aircraft that had taken part in the feint had crossed the narrow strip of Norway toward Narvik that the observers in the squadron leader's plotting office noticed that 29 machines were missing from the total of more than 50, just as the German fighters, completely bewildered, were landing again and asking what was happening.

Simultaneously the Lancasters were dropping their six-ton superheavy bombs on the last German battleship. *Ensom Dronning—Solitary Queen*—was what the Norwegians called the *Tirpitz*, and solitary she remained in her death throes. Unconquered at sea, but chained to her berth by lack of fuel, it was to be her fate to be destroyed piecemeal by the unremitting attacks of ever-renewed swarms of enemies from the air.

Shortly after 9:00 A.M. on November 12 the order "Action stations!" sounded all through the *Tirpitz*. The ship's radar had picked up the enemy aircraft at a distance of 50 miles and was plotting their course as they flew straight along the Tromsö Fjord toward their target. When they arrived at a distance of seventeen and a half miles, the commander ordered the main armament to open fire. For the last time the mighty barrels of the 15-inch guns were raised and spat fire at the enemy, who was flying in at a great height. One after the other, the lighter guns joined in, but the heavy four-engine bombers continued unflinchingly on their set course.

Then the bombs began to come down; the men at the guns could see them distinctly, plopping down almost playfully as the British blanketed the ship with death and destruction. Two direct hits, one on the 15-inch gun-turret "Caesar" and one on one of the magazines, and ten near hits immediately alongside sealed the doom of the *Solitary Queen*. She heeled over to starboard quite slowly, still firing all her guns. When the starboard side of the upper deck was already sliding into the water and the sailors could barely hold on any longer, the doors and ammunition hoists had jammed, and all firing had had to cease, the commander gave his last order:

"Abandon ship!"

He himself and the officers cooped up with him in the armored conning tower could do nothing to save themselves. The heavy steel door was jammed, and no human power could open it. The German captain and his officers went down with the sinking *Tirpitz*, and approximately 1400 seamen, who either failed to get clear of the ship or were killed by bombs, shared their fate.

Three hundred and ninety-seven men were saved, and more than 400 members of the crew were not aboard at the time of the disaster. Two Messerschmitt fighters pursued—when it was too late—the departing enemy squadron and shot down seven British machines in the space of a few minutes before they were obliged to turn back.

14

Supporting the Eastern Front

AT MIDNIGHT AUGUST 20, 1944, A HEAVY CRUISER steamed through the Irben road between Courland and the island of Sarema. She moved almost without a sound, her lights were dimmed, and her course was east, toward the front.

In this case it was the front line of the armies fighting on land, for at sea the front was everywhere. The ship was liable to strike a mine at any moment, which could have been dropped by Soviet aircraft weeks or only hours ago. She might also be attacked by submarines at any moment, although this was an eventuality with which the staff no longer reckoned seriously, as no Russian submarines had been sighted in the Baltic outside the blocked Bay of Finland since 1942. It was to be expected, however, that Red bombers and fighters would attack as soon as it was daylight, and the ship's antiaircraft guns of all calibers were prepared to give them a warm reception.

The big ship, screened on all sides by an escort of four destroyers and five torpedo boats, was the cruiser *Prinz Eugen*, which was to support the German Army in the East with her gunfire.

Toward 3:00 A.M. everybody on board the *Prinz,* as the crew called their ship, was sent to action stations. Now her decks were cleared she was ready to engage in battle at a moment's notice. Course was set well into the Bay of Riga. At that point the Russians had broken through to the coast some time ago, with an armored wedge 20 to 25 miles wide, thus cutting off the German garrison of Riga from the German front in Courland. A counterattack by German tank divisions was now planned in order to re-establish communications with Riga. As the army artillery was not strong enough to prepare the attack sufficiently, it was to be reinforced by naval gunfire.

On August 20 at 7:00 A.M. the cruiser fired her first ranging shots. The gunnery officer was in constant telephone communication by ultrashort wave with the carrier aircraft acting as spotter and hovering above the target area, as well as with advanced army observation posts and the spearhead of the German tank units. The target, invisible from the cruiser, was the town of Tukums, situated some 15 miles inland, a railway junction where the Russian opposition had stiffened.

When the *Prinz Eugen* had fired the first round from her 8-inch guns, a confusion of voices came through the ultrashort-wave set:

"Bravo! Plumb on the target! Donnerwetter, you're delivering the goods! Heavy stuff, this! Go on. . . ."

They were all talking at once. The cruiser had to beg them to moderate their enthusiasm. As she continued to fire round after round, the observers gave 80 per cent as direct hits. The cruiser was not even firing from a fixed position, but steaming to and fro. Nevertheless there was no doubt the *Prinz* was firing with great accuracy.

Meanwhile the German destroyers also were intervening in the battle on land, their medium guns doing good work. When the garrison of Riga made a sortie in order to break through to the tanks, the Russians, who had evidently been taken by surprise by the intervention of the warships, did nothing whatever in the way of counterattacking. Though the *Prinz Eugen* was on the alert for attacks by the Soviet Air Force, not one enemy aircraft appeared; as the lookouts searched sky and water in vain, the bombardment continued unhindered.

Late in the afternoon the Army sent a message of thanks for effective support. The Russian opposition seemed to be broken, and for the time being the support of the heavy naval gunfire was no longer needed. The cruiser steamed rapidly out of Riga Bay, so as to avoid a last-minute attack, for the *Prinz* would have been extremely vulnerable in these narrow and shallow waters. However, she returned to Gotenhaven (Gdynia) without difficulty and was immediately made ready to sail again.

The success of this first "live" shoot after months and years of training gave a new incentive to the crews of the ships that made up the remainder of the German fleet in the Baltic. With the exception of one attack from the air, the *Prinz Eugen,* for instance, had not noticed the war for more than two years. Other ships had been stationed in the Baltic even longer, as they had to be used as training ships for both officers and men, especially crews for the steadily increasing number of U boats. Since Hitler had decided that the "tin boxes" were no longer any use, and were to be put out of commission, the Fleet Training Squadron had been strengthened. By this move, the OKM had saved many a great ship from self-destruction, as even Hitler approved of them as training ships. Except for short periods when they were used in Norway, the following ships constituted the training squadron: the old battleships *Schlesien* and *Schleswig Holstein,* the armored ships *Admiral Scheer* and *Lützow* and the heavy cruiser *Prinz Eugen,* the light cruisers *Nürnberg, Leipzig, Köln,* and *Emden,* and among various others three sail training ships.

Officers and men in these ships, which represented quite a formidable fighting unit, were often bitterly disappointed at the passive role they had to play, forced as they were to do peaceful training work in the quiet waters of the Baltic, while the war was raging with increasing fury on all fronts, and not least at sea.

However, the Naval Staff was well aware of the importance of adequate training and did not allow itself to be deflected from this principle even during 1943 and 1944. Early in 1944 it became increasingly evident that the Russians were becoming dangerous enemies in the Baltic. The intervention of the *Prinz Eugen* at Riga had been an undoubted success. A sigh of relief went up from the Army General Staff—one could fight with one's back to the sea all right, when the ships were there to support one with their heavy guns. Thus a fighting squadron of especially effective warships was detached from the training squadron, and suddenly what remained of the Baltic fleet found itself faced with an important task. At first this was only to consist in supporting the troops on land, but all too soon it developed into holding up the Russian advance again and again, so as to allow as many men, women, and children as possible to escape from the Red invasion toward the west. Hundreds of thousands of Germans today are indebted to the incessant work of all types of ships for their life and liberty.

Thanks to the intervention of heavy naval guns between October 10 and 23, 1944, the city of Memel, its defenders, its inhabitants, and the refugees who had sought sanctuary there did not fall into the hands of the Russians then attacking in strength. The ships took turns in bombarding the attacking forces. But when the *Prinz Eugen* hurried back to Gotenhaven on October 15 to replenish her ammunition, an unexpected catastrophe occurred.

That same day the cruiser *Leipzig* sailed from Gotenhaven at dusk. After a training that had lasted six months, she too was to be given an active belligerent task, namely, that of embarking a few hundred mines at Swinemünde.

The sky was overcast and dusk fell rapidly as the *Leipzig* steamed around the Hela Peninsula in order to gain the open sea. At 7:50 P.M. the engineers received the order to uncouple the diesel engines, which were only used at half-speed, from the propeller shafts and to connect up the turbines. This meant that the cruiser must remain for a little time with her engines stopped. The night was very dark and there was a dense fog. One could see barely 50 yards ahead. The *Leipzig* had put out all her lights, as Russian submarines had been reported, and dozens of men were peering out anxiously into the surrounding darkness as the lonely ship drifted on without her engines.

At 8:00 P.M. 100 cadets stepped through the small bulkhead out of their sleeping quarters which had originally been No. 2 engine room and had been destroyed by a mine in December, 1939. When the repairs were carried out it had been converted into a dormitory for a hundred seamen.

As the *Leipzig* was now at cruising stations, half the crew took over the watch from the other half every four hours. The hundred cadets were to take over at 8:00 P.M. The minutes went by. Any minute now the engines would be connected up again and the cruiser steam on its way.

At that moment—it was exactly four minutes past eight—a terrible shock went through the ship.

Two ship's carpenters were sitting in their workshop between the bridge and the funnel on the upper deck, playing chess. Precisely at 8:04 P.M. their game was disturbed by a third party. The two men saw with horror the starboard bulwark of their workshop split from end to end with a deafening crash. Something that looked like the bow of a gigantic ship thrust itself between them, clearing both of them by the fraction of an inch. And it actually was the bow of a ship that had overturned their chessboard—the bow of a 10,000-ton cruiser. A second later the workshop collapsed, but the two carpenters remained miraculously unharmed and were able to crawl out from under the debris.

The terrific impact plunged the ship into total darkness, even the emergency lighting ceasing to function. The crew picked themselves up as best they could out of the corners into which they had been hurled, while the officer in the control room scribbled blindly in his logbook:

"8:04 P.M. Hit by torpedo."

Only one means of communication had remained intact: the voice pipe to the bridge, and through this he discovered his error. The executive officer shouted down:

"*Prinz Eugen* has hit us, *Prinz Eugen* has rammed us!"

The heavy cruiser also had received a submarine warning and had been similarly steaming through the night and the fog with all her lights out. It was too late to avoid the collision when the other ship suddenly appeared in front of her bows like a phantom. The engines were immediately rung astern, but it was too late.

The *Prinz* had thrust her sharp bow with all her might into the *Leipzig* exactly amidships, on the starboard side between the bridge and the funnel. The crew of the antiaircraft guns standing there were literally pulped. With a rending sound, the bow sliced through the cruiser to the central keel plate, thus literally cutting her through to the middle, so that it was to be feared that her back might break at any moment.

In No. 3 engine room the entire technical personnel was scalded by the steam escaping from the shattered boilers. No. 2 engine room was filled with sea water within 20 seconds—the ward where only a quarter of an hour earlier 100 cadets had been sleeping peacefully. Four minutes earlier the last of them had stepped out of it, their lives saved by the changing of the watch.

The bows of the *Prinz Eugen* stood open like the jaws of a shark, between whose teeth the *Leipzig* was hanging helplessly. Inextricably locked together, the two cruisers thus drifted in the waters of the Baltic for 14 hours, within range of Russian submarines and aircraft. Had they been in British waters, both ships would certainly have been lost, but the Russians did not attack.

In the meantime radio messages had been sent out and tugs and other craft arrived on the scene. Two tugs with 16 pumps set about pumping the water out of the fo'c'sle of the *Leipzig* as rapidly as possible, so as to keep the cruiser afloat. For the time being she was still hanging from the bows of the *Prinz Eugen* and being carried along by her big brother. But what would happen if they succeeded in disentangling the two ships? Yet the attempt had to be made. The maneuver was prepared for by the use of welding torches. The crew of the *Leipzig* were taken off and put on board the other ships, leaving only the key officers and ratings on board. They had already inflated their life jackets, ready to jump overboard at any moment.

Toward 10:00 A.M., 14 hours after the collision, the 133,000-HP engines of the *Prinz Eugen* drove her astern, while the tugs held the *Leipzig* stationary. All would be well if she did not break in two—and stand firm she did. The bow of the *Prinz Eugen* was withdrawn from her shattered side, the ships were clear of each other, and both remained afloat.

In this way the heavy cruiser reached the security of Goten-haven docks under her own steam, the light cruiser with the assistance of the tugs. A fortnight later the *Prinz Eugen* had been fully repaired, but the hole in the *Leipzig* could only be temporarily patched up. Even so, she continued to carry on. Long after the end of the war the British sank her in the North Sea together with a cargo of poison gas.

Unaffected by the disaster of Hela, the other ships of the "Thiele fighting-squadron," so named after its admiral, continued to intervene in the battles on land wherever the situation appeared threatening. On November 18, 1914, after a heavy preliminary 12-hour bombardment of the peninsula of Sõrvemaa, which pushes out to sea like a long finger at the south end of Sarema, the Russians advanced to attack the main German front. The Germans were unable to send reinforcements to Sõrvemaa in order to halt the superior forces of the enemy, but, although the peninsula had to be given up, it was hoped to save the troops and their valuable equipment. This could only be done by halting the Russian advance, and the heavy naval guns had thus to intervene, so as to permit the troops on land to disengage from the enemy. Admiral Thiele sailed to the battle area with the *Prinz Eugen,* which had meanwhile been repaired, and the armored ship *Lützow.*

The salvos from the turrets of both ships reached their targets with terrifying precision. After a day and a half, however, they had used up their available ammunition, but the *Admiral*

Scheer and *Admiral Hipper* had appeared on the scene to relieve them, and by this means the naval bombardment of the targets on the peninsula was able to continue almost without a break.

This was no longer nearly as easy as it had been in August, during that first bombardment of Tukums. From day to day the Russians were becoming increasingly conscious of the heavy damage and the great loss of life inflicted on them by the German ships, so they were using every means in their power to destroy these dangerous opponents. When their 17-cm. batteries engaged the ships from the land, the cruisers went further out to sea—the range of their own heavy guns being sufficient to outrange the enemy's. The Russians then attacked simultaneously with whole squadrons of torpedo aircraft and high-altitude bombers. Turning and twisting wildly, the *Admiral Scheer*—obviously the main target of the Russians with her powerful 11-inch guns—tried to avoid the massed attack. Heavy bombs were falling all around her, and more than once she was covered by sea water, which gushed up in high fountains breaking on the decks. The Germans were being given a foretaste of what they would have to expect in every subsequent action—a testimony to the respect in which the Russians held them. But neither bombs nor torpedoes found their mark.

A further tribute to the ships' effectiveness was the fact that the troops on Sõrvemaa were able to withdraw in good order. Their commanders sent plain-language radio messages to their comrades at sea, expressing their thanks. Thiele smiled happily. For two whole years he had been forced to use his ships in the Baltic for training exercises, and now he knew that the time had not been wasted, as was proved to him even more strikingly by the enthusiastic descriptions of army observers over the ultra-short wave.

In the meanwhile, the Russians were attempting with gunboats and light craft of all kinds to prevent the Germans from taking their troops off the peninsula, but they were met by furious resistance from German mine sweepers, frigates, and gunboats. These small units were part of the 9th Salvage Division. Under their protection the German troops and most of their equipment were ferried across to Courland in naval landing barges. On the morning of November 25 the Red divisions advanced to the furthest ends of the peninsula, but they were attacking into the void, for the Germans had gone, leaving nothing behind except a few small stranded wrecks.

A week or two later the *Admiral Scheer* returned again to her base at Gotenhaven. Hardly had she been made fast to the jetty when the sentries noticed a few soldiers hesitantly approaching the ship. They were all bandaged—it was a party of slightly wounded men on their way home.

"Well, what do you want?" someone called down from the decks.

"Were you there at Sõrvemaa?" the soldiers shouted back.

"Of course. What about it?"

Instead of answering, the soldiers started to scramble up the gangway. Then they wrung the hands of the surprised seamen with tears of joy in their eyes.

"Thank you," was all they could say. "Thank you!"

A circle had formed around the strange group; questions and answers followed each other. The crew of the *Admiral Scheer* were delighted to receive a firsthand description of the efficacy of their intervention. The troops had in fact just arrived from Sõrvemaa.

"We'd already given up the idea of getting out of there. And then you started dropping your big stuff. . . ."

At the same time the supreme commander of the German Navy, Grossadmiral Dönitz, forwarded the text of a signal he had received from the C.-in-C. of the Army to the ships that had been involved. It went as follows:

On terminating the action on Sõrvemaa, I feel myself impelled to ask you to convey my thanks and that of the entire Army of the East to all members of the Navy for the eminent and self-sacrificing support they have given us. I am convinced that our united struggle against overwhelmingly superior enemy forces has linked the bonds of comradeship between the Navy and the Army even more closely.

Guderian, General

In mid-January, 1945, the German light cruiser *Emden* went alongside the Schichau wharf in Königsberg harbor. The *Emden* was the first medium-sized ship built by the German Reich's Navy after the First World War.

Her engines needed overhauling now; but for days an uncanny stillness had brooded over the cruiser. The riveters' hammers were silent; the cranes stood idle; the yard's brisk hum had given place to a paralyzed immobility. Only in the distance the deep, growling thunder of the guns could be heard, where the Russians were attacking. By January 19 the situation had become so acute that there was a headlong conscription of all workers into the Volksturm (Home Guard), to be concentrated around the capital of East Prussia. The "Fortress of Königsberg" was to be defended.

Since then the Schichau dockyard had fallen silent. Everything in the *Emden* lay about, just as the last shift of workers had left it in their sudden departure; the upper deck was strewn with engine parts and other spares and tools. The crew regarded the confusion in some dismay. What was going to happen now? What would the *Emden's* next move be?

Meanwhile the thunder of the guns was sufficient evidence that the front was daily drawing closer.

On January 23 the executive officer and deputy commander of the *Emden,* Fregattenkapitän Wickmann, at last received an urgent telephone call from Berlin, direct from the OKM. The cruiser was to prepare to go to sea at once; an icebreaker had been ordered; with the help of tugs the ship was to be passed through the Königsberg Canal as far as Pillau; under her own steam the *Emden* could do some five knots—the first officer must move her to Kiel where the engine overhauling could be completed.

While preparations for leaving the yard were in full swing, another call came through from Berlin. The *Emden* would have to wait a bit; she was not to move from the jetty until a valuable cargo had arrived and been stowed on board: the coffins of Field Marshal and Reichs President Von Hindenburg and his wife Gertrud.

A few hours before the first Russian armored divisions had reached the Tannenberg Memorial a captain of the Pioneer Corps there had loaded the coffins onto two heavy trucks which were now on their way to Königsberg. Of the few routes to the west which remained open that by the sea was the safest. Meanwhile hundreds of sailors had been striving to bring some order into the confusion in the *Emden*. A part of the upper deck of the cruiser had been cleared, and here the first officer had the cork lifesaving gear piled up, rampart-wise, in an oval, leaving a free space in the center for the coffins.

Hour after hour went by. The ship lay ready to go to sea, her dock already flooded and the icebreaker in position. With the approach of night snow began to fall continuously in great thick flakes which smothered every sound. At about 10:00 P.M. a car drove up and a general got out and came on board—Oscar von Hindenburg, son of the marshal. He wanted to take leave of his parents here, not knowing whether he would survive the coming weeks in Königsberg. (He did survive, and had a chance to see the coffins again, when the Americans came upon them in August, 1946, after following many false trails, and had them buried together with those of Frederick William I and Frederick II in the Elisabeth Church in Marburg.)

Apart from a few brief telephone calls the crew of the *Emden* had had no indication of the time of arrival of the convoy. Midnight was long past, and it was bitterly cold on board, for the present state of the cruiser did not permit her to be heated. At long last there was a sign of life as at three o'clock in the morning the trucks drove on to the jetty.

It was a quiet, peaceful night—there might have been no war and no Russians lying in wait. The white sheet of fresh-fallen snow covered everything and still the great flakes came down. In no time they had formed themselves into furry tufts on the caps and shoulders of the score of seamen who were acting as guard of honor. Ancient flags and standards from the Tannenberg Memorial hung from the wall of lifesaving gear as, in the dim light of the arc lamps, the heavy bronze sarcophagi—over six feet long as they were and almost three wide—were hoisted by crane from jetty to ship, slowly swinging down into their small temporary court of honor. Only the most necessary commands were given, and those in a hushed voice.

At four in the morning the *Emden* slipped from the jetty and, with her icebreaker towing, set out for Pillau, leaving Königsberg behind. Was it not symbolic for the last months of the war —the victor of 1914 fleeing from the victor of 1945? Hindenburg had abandoned East Prussia.

In December, 1944, the German Baltic fleet lost the old battleship *Schleswig Holstein,* sunk after a bombing attack outside Gotenhaven, but from January, 1945, onward the heavy cruisers had again been taking a hand in the land war. The need now was to save the garrison of Memel, eager to make their way through to Samland via the Kurische Nehrung, the tongue of sandhills between the Baltic and the Bay of Courland. In spite of Russian attempts to cut them off by pushing to the sea at Cranz, the heavy gunfire from the ships stopped them and succeeded in keeping the Cranz gap open for a considerable time, as thousands of soldiers and fugitives streamed daily through this last safety gap into the one remaining corner of Samland that still held out.

Their goal was Pillau, from which they hoped to go by sea further westward. But the innumerable hosts of refugees could not possibly all be contained in the small seaport town, and terrible scenes ensued. Naval and merchant shipping did what they could to cope with the situation, but when the ships were rushed there, nothing could be done but put off from the jetty as the Russian armies were encircling the town. The link with

Königsberg was broken because the Russians had managed to push their way through to the Frisches Haff. Once again the *Lützow* and *Admiral Scheer* sent salvos far over Pillau into the enemy's lines, with the result that the Army succeeded, at the second attempt, in opening for a few more days the connecting link between Königsberg and Pillau, and once more the endless lines of fugitives streamed out of the capital toward Pillau, the spot which to them spelled the last chance of safety.

Through the range finder of the *Admiral Scheer* more long black treks were to be seen moving across the frozen Haff—people, animals, and cars here and there breaking through the ice. The Russian artillery added their quota to the general misery, and the watching seamen could but long to receive more fuel and ammunition soon, so that their guns would be able to "talk" again. But the prospects for both oil and shells were pretty grim. By early February, however, the ships' guns were able to provide some breathing space for the army which was slowly being forced into the gulf at Elbing, Tolkemit, and Frauenburg.

In this action the guns of the *Admiral Scheer* fired at a range of 22 miles into the Russian lines, the greatest range at which they had ever been used. The rifling was worn smooth and the cruiser had to sail to Kiel to have new liners put in there. The ship left Gotenhaven for Kiel at the beginning of March with 800 refugees and 200 wounded men on board in addition to her own crew. But even with this throng of passengers she was able to give some help in the land battle. Between Kolberg and Dievenow the long line of refugees, winding its way under the coast, was again being subjected to the Russian artillery. *Admiral Scheer* reacted three times with such powerful gunfire that the Russians were silenced.

In the meantime the English air reconnaissance had become so effective that they at once identified the German "pocket battleship" in Kiel dockyard, where their bombing attacks were a daily and nightly occurrence. The *Admiral Scheer* was lucky until April 9 and even in the raid which started at 10:00 P.M. that night it seemed at first as if this luck would hold. After a hail of bombs lasting for 20 minutes the ship had still escaped a direct hit. Then, however, a stick of bombs fell into the water close against her side and, exploding, tore away the whole of her side plating. She heeled over with a lurch and sank within a few minutes.

The majority of the crew found shelter in a bunker on land. Of the care and maintenance party on board a small number, together with the commander, managed to scramble onto the outer plating and so reach safety. Thirty-two seamen met their death in this furious attack.

Such was the end of the *Admiral Scheer,* the only big ship of the Navy to be duly and correctly buried. For when the war was over the berth where she lay was filled in with rubble. People can now walk over it, but only a very few of them have any idea that one of the armored ships of the German Navy lies buried beneath their feet.

At the same time the heavy cruiser *Admiral Hipper* received a severe hit when in dry dock at Kiel, so Admiral Thiele was left with only two ships at his disposal as a fighting squadron—the *Lützow* and the *Prinz Eugen.* Since March 23 both these ships had been ceaselessly engaged in the fighting round Danzig and Gotenhaven. As the Russian ring around this latter great naval focal point was being drawn tighter and tighter, the ships' guns had the task of providing a little more air and breathing space for the sorely pressed land forces, as they had already done so often in the previous months. Countless thousands of fugitives, soldiers, wounded, women, and children were also in this town. The Navy again collected all its resources for an immense transport effort. Even from Norway ships were sent for in order to rescue people from the Russians.

As Gotenhaven Roads lay in sparkling spring sunshine the lines of merchant shipping, come to cast anchor there, stretched as far as the eye could reach. Several times a day Russian fighter-bombers of the IL-2 type attacked the German cruisers whose artillery kept the Russian front under constant fire. In spite of recklessly daring assaults by these aircraft, however, the ships were lucky, and none of the bombs hit their target. All fell into the sea and the bombers' only success was to leave, after their attacks, miles of dead fish drifting, belly upward, on the surface.

During the first days of April, however, the land position became untenable. In the night between the seventh and eighth of that month naval troop-carrying vessels ferried some 30,000 infantrymen out of Gotenhaven. With the town's surrender the peninsula of Hela was all that remained as a last German rallying point in the Bay of Danzig.

In the meantime the heavy cruiser *Lützow* sailed westward and anchored off Swinemünde, where Admiral Thiele, head of the fighting squadron, was expected for an inspection on the evening of April 16. But as it turned out this inspection never took place.

Shortly after 5:00 P.M. the men were sitting at their evening meal, thoroughly enjoying the rest which was doubly welcome after their sleepless days and nights off Gotenhaven. The radio program from the ship's loud-speaker could be heard from one of the cabins. The news had just ended and the air-warning announcements wound up with:

"Approximately 18 four-engined bombers over the Mecklenburg area."

"Well, boys, I'll be darned if that isn't pretty near us here," commented one of the seamen as they sat and gazed at each other.

Only a bare minute later came a message over the ship's loud-speaker:

"Heavy flak close up!" it went, and after a short pause: *"All the flak you have close up!"*

With the sound of men's clattering, trampling feet as they hurried to their guns there now mingled suddenly the barking of the light flak from destroyers in the vicinity of the *Lützow*. At once the alarm bell shrilled through the cruiser. The men left on the mess decks sprang to close the armored deadlights over the scuttles—but several of them never got so far.

Suddenly a great quivering shock went through the ship—then a second, duller thud—and immediately a third.

The English group consisted of special Lancaster aircraft for attacking marine targets. In November, 1944, six-ton bombs had destroyed the *Tirpitz* and these same six-ton bombs were now destroying the *Lützow*—a ship only a quarter the *Tirpitz's* size. The men's quarters, where they had been having supper only five minutes before, were now in utter chaos, and the ladders to the upper decks were torn away. As sailors and cadets pulled themselves, aching, to their feet—the ship listing heavily to port —from somewhere or other there was a shout:

"Get on deck, we're sinking!"

Thick reddish-brown smoke billowed out to meet the men now hurriedly seeking a way out to safety. The *Lützow* was heeling over more than ever on her side. In this oblique position her bows protruded queerly from the water, while the quarter-deck was many feet lower and in parts already awash. One bomb had dropped into the marshy ground between ship and land and splashed a fountain of black, sticky slime over the ship, through which the men were now wading ankle-deep. Some slipped and slid against the guard rail; others, missing even that support, fell into the black mess from which it was almost impossible to extricate themselves. But there was no time now to bother with these unfortunates.

All hands abandon ship—except flak and damage-control personnel!

Already a second wave of bombers could be seen approaching. Hundreds were still swimming in the water or running to take cover in the nearby woods when the next series of heavy bombs exploded round the ship.

Then all was quiet round the *Lützow* and after a quarter of an hour the crew ventured to return. The cruiser, listing heavily to port, lay on the very flat bed of the "Kaiserfahrt." A bomb had flung the top end of the mast together with the radio aerials and the armored director into the water. Other bombs exploding close to her port side had torn a huge hole in it and this caused the *Lützow* to sink. The actual hits among those six-ton bombs had struck the ship directly forward of turret "Anton" and a bit sideways from turret "Bruno"—in other words, close to the 11-inch guns.

But both bombs were duds! The rear one lay in the shell room of turret "Bruno." If it had exploded along with the 500 shells stowed there, the cruiser would have been blown to atoms and probably none of the crew would have survived. As it happened, however, the losses were astonishingly small: under 20 killed and another score wounded—all soldiers who had been on the upper deck when the bombs came.

Eleven days later a great deal had been done to the *Lützow*. Great wedges of timber had been hewn and inserted in order to close up the underwater leaks in her side. A salvage vessel had managed, through successive processes of clearing and flooding, to raise the vessel from its crooked position so that it now lay straight on the canal bottom. More could not be done; the *Lützow* would never float again. The engineers were released from service, the flak crew likewise, though the latter, with their guns, would find plenty to do on the land front. The rest of the crew remained in the ship. The dud bomb in turret "Anton" was successfully disposed of. As one of the electric generators was again functioning it was possible for the forward 11-inch turret and the medium armament to fire once more.

Such was the position early in the morning of April 28 when the alarm bell rang out again in the darkness, waking the crew from their short, heavy sleep. Turret "Anton" was firing whatever its liners permitted. The Russians had broken through at Pasewalk at 4:00 A.M. and were now pushing north to the coast. *Lützow* was taking a hand in the fight with her main armament, although only her superstructure was above water.

In the night of May 1–2 a new alarm rang out over the decks of the *Lützow:*

Abandon ship! Ship on fire!

Flames had broken out in the only electric generating set which still functioned. There was a big risk of explosions: the fire might burn its way through to the stocks of 5.9-inch ammunition; it might also set afire the fuel oil lying deep in the interior of the ship. In constant danger of their lives, the men began rolling away the shells lying near the seat of the fire, until, warned by the bursting flak ammunition, they were forced to retire. Scarcely had they taken cover in the woods when explosion after explosion roared over their heads, coming from the 5.9-inch shells.

The morning sun shone upon a dismal sight. There lay the ship, a rusty red color, with a thin spiral of smoke issuing from a funnel. The upper deck was scarred and shell-torn. The fire had been especially fierce in the forward part of the ship. Even turret "Anton" was now unable to fire any more, the electrical power having failed.

The last remaining members of the crew took leave of their ship on May 3, when a motorboat transported them to Swinemünde. But there fresh orders awaited them:

All medium armament guns' crews back to the ship.

In an ammunition store in the vicinity 3000 rounds of 5.9-inch ammunition had been found, which were to be fired from the ship against the advancing Russians.

One of those who went back on board that last time has given his account of the closing hours of the *Lützow:*

"When we noticed a flicker of machine-gun fire east of Caseburg as darkness fell, we were pretty sure that the Russians would be along before next morning. At 22:15 hours came the expected order:

"Prepare ship for demolition!

"Every gun had a shell placed in reverse in its barrel. Turret 'Bruno' was well filled with 5.9-inch shells, cartridges, and other explosive material. All the fuses were concentrated on the starboard side. Around midnight the engines of the small vessel which accommodated the sorely overcrowded crew started up.

" 'All clear?' the executive officer asked. 'Let's go; I'm lighting the fuses.'

"Then he sprang across and we moved off, gazing backward in silence. We had proceeded about a mile downriver, when at 12 minutes after midnight on May 4, 1945, on both port and starboard sides of the *Lützow* huge craters of fire gaped open and sheets of flame began flaring out into the night. But what had happened to turret 'Bruno'? We began to think something must have gone wrong when a gigantic tongue of fire shot straight up into the sky and a heartbeat later a terrific explosion blasted our ears and we distinctly felt the atmospheric pressure. Our job was done. Those guns had fired their last round. . . ."

Such was the end of the armored ship *Lützow*, the former *Deutschland*, which, already sunk by the English, nevertheless continued to the last moment firing at the Russians.

15

The Last Battle

MEANWHILE THE BALTIC WAS BUZZING WITH RADIO messages. Two of them, dispatched by the Admiral Eastern Baltic, who from his bunker on Hela Peninsula was in charge of the returning transports and was endeavoring to maintain order, in their laconic way gave a clear enough indication of the state of affairs. The first went:

Most secret. A total of 225,000 soldiers and 25,000 fugitives is to be convoyed from area AOK East Prussia; 175,000 of these already on Hela. Rest still in Vistula flats.

Except for Courland, the narrow peninsula of Hela was the last German rallying point in the east, to the tip of which everyone with the faintest hope of escaping the Russians was now flocking. Since the fall of Gotenhaven Russian batteries had stationed themselves on the opposite shore near Oxhöft and were firing across at Hela. Fighters and fighter-bombers were also almost perpetually over the peninsula, dropping their bombs into the crowds and interfering with the activities of small craft in Danzig Bay.

For there was still something like a German front in the Vistula flats, between the mouths of the Vistula and Nogat rivers and on the Frische Nehrung, and if at all possible this had to be maintained until the last man and the last woman had been transported to Hela. Night after night innumerable small—even diminutive—craft set out on this big transport job. With dimmed lights they stole out over Danzig Bay, and scarcely had they approached the shore anywhere on the mainland coast before hundreds—indeed thousands—of poor creatures waded out to meet them. Others, unable to walk themselves—wounded, old, and infirm—were hoisted onto the sailors' backs and carried to the boats, often sinking nearly up to their necks before a rescuing line was thrown to them.

At several points on the Nehrung emergency piers were constructed, where the small craft might come alongside. During the daylight hours Russian aircraft would come and drop bombs on them, but at night the damage was always made good. Boat after boat would come up and in no time be filled to capacity with escaping people and cross over to the peninsula, only to return once more to the mainland . . . this went on all night, the small craft plying to and fro, to take the innumerable crowds still pushing on board. Hela meant the first step to freedom. Once there one might get farther on. But how? There would be time to think about that when one had got there.

How serious the position actually was became evident from the second radio message dispatched by Thiele on Hela to the OKM:

Owing to almost complete stoppage of Baltic convoy traffic to Hela over 200,000 people massed here in short time. Have avoided all appearance of impending collapse. Request immediate large-scale provision ship space for transport away. Steamer to the west only May 2 and 3. Assistance urgently necessary.

Up to this moment the Navy had already transported a million and a half persons to the west—from Memel, Pillau, Danzig, Gotenhaven, and now Hela. In every way possible the ships tried to do their best for the masses of refugees crowding the ports, possessed often with one terror only—that at the last minute the Russians would overtake them.

But the Russians were lying in wait for them out at sea also. Now that the German blockade of the Gulf of Finland had been lifted they kept sending their submarines out to harass the convoy traffic across the Baltic. So it was not all plain sailing for the transports. The torpedoing and sinking of the three big ships *Wilhelm Gustloff, General von Steuben,* and *Goya* represented in each case a catastrophe in which thousands of refugees and wounded were sacrificed. After weeks of hardship during their winter flight those unfortunate souls had scarcely plucked up a little courage again on board the ships when these literally gave way beneath their feet and they were plunged into the icy water. In the *Goya* disaster everything happened so quickly that out of a total of 6000 on board fewer than 200 could be saved.

Yet, in spite of that, compared with the hundreds of thousands who managed to get away from the danger zone, the losses were small. After the *Goya* went down these still amounted to only .49 per cent of the numbers rescued during the period in question.

But what was happening now? Why had no more transports come to Hela in the last two days, with the waiting crowds growing and growing? Why was it necessary for the Admiral Eastern Baltic command to demand shipping so urgently? Couldn't the Navy do anything any more—or was it that there was a shortage of oil fuel?

On that third of May other things were claiming the attention of the German Navy. Chief among them was the "Rainbow" order. A radio message from the OKM explains what this meant:

The fundamental order remains in force that battleships, cruisers, destroyers, torpedo boats, E dispatch vessels, U boats, and small combat vessels shall not fall into the hands of the enemy, but on receipt of the code word "Rainbow" are to be sunk or otherwise destroyed.

This code word "Rainbow" might be given at any moment. While the Americans and the Russians were trying to outstrip each other in central Germany, the English were pushing northward to the ports. If the ships and boats of the Navy were not to fall into their hands, they would have to scuttle themselves.

Against this background there came the cry for help from the east where the hopes of over 250,000 Germans in the Hela area and, over and above them, 100,000 soldiers in the extreme north of Courland were fixed on those very ships which meant for them a chance of salvation.

On the evening of May 2 Grossadmiral Dönitz sent Admiral von Friedeburg and other naval and army officers from Kiel to the British Headquarters on the Lüneburger Heath. At noon the following day they were received by Field Marshal Montgomery. As soon as the latter had heard Dönitz's offer of capitulation he gave orders that the air attacks, fixed for the next day, were not to take place. When Von Friedeburg returned to his superior officer he brought with him, in addition to other capitulation demands of Montgomery's, the following:

"All ships still afloat in the northern capitulation area, including Holland and Denmark, are to be handed over to the Allies."

Dönitz accepted these conditions. Had he not done so then the concentrated bombing attacks on the few towns still in German possession would have continued. Had he not done so, the Allies would have refused to let the hundreds of thousands of troops and fugitives, streaming back from the east, pass through their own lines and these hundreds of thousands would thus at the last moment have passed into Russian captivity.

It may well have been bitter for the Admiral to be obliged to hand over his ships, seeing that it had been the rule hitherto to sink them before they fell into the enemy's hands. The last example of this kind was given by the French in 1942 when they destroyed their Navy at the last moment before the surprise advance of the Germans toward Toulon. But for Dönitz there was no other way. When he was later asked in prison at Nürnberg why he had canceled the "Rainbow" order he replied:

"In view of the magnitude of the collapse it was merely a question of halting the bloodshed and of rescuing as many Germans as possible from the Russians. Certainly the ships had to be handed over, but honor had really been satisfied. I therefore capitulated."

Once again the radio messages went chasing each other over the Baltic, but they had now somewhat changed their tune. On the morning of May 5 the order went out from the OKW:

Hostilities against English and Americans to cease immediately.

All mine sweepers, torpedo boats, dispatch vessels, as well as the steamers Linz, Ceuta, Pompeii, *at present lying in Copenhagen, to start immediately for the east to assist in evacuation; also the auxiliary cruiser* Hansa. *Report to Eastern Naval Command; port of destination to be announced by radio.*

For Hela, Lepaya, Ventspils, and Bornholm: as from May 5, 08:00 hours, German summertime, armistice in regard to troops of Field Marshal Montgomery. Transports at sea to continue on their way, Navy's task to rescue Germans from the east. Engage in no destructive activity, sinking of ships, or other demonstration. Insure safety of stores.

All of which meant the cancellation of "Rainbow." In almost every instance the action taken was in keeping with the new state of affairs. Only the U boat arm refused to believe that such an order could represent the genuine desire of the Grossadmiral and have been issued without coercion. In the night of May 4–5, shortly before the capitulation to the English came into force, all German U boats in Baltic and North Sea harbors were therefore sunk. For the rest of the Navy, however, there was now another task—to save all that could be saved. Everything that could float now made its way over the Baltic to meet the waiting thousands there. From the 10,000-ton *Hansa* to the smallest harbor tug, if only they had the fuel necessary for the trip, they all took part in this race against time. For at the very moment the capitulation, which involved the Russians too, came into force, the latter would clearly penetrate to the harbors and put a stop to any further evacuations, be they from Hela, Ventspils, or Lepaya.

Early on May 7 some evacuation numbers were given over the radio. According to this report some 43,000 people were shipped from Hela alone on May 6, not including those who put out to sea in small or very small boats on their own account.

Forty-three thousand souls in one day! But many times that number were still waiting on the peninsula. Theoretically it would take a week to rescue the lot, so Dönitz made every effort to have the final capitulation date postponed. However, on the same day, a radio message gave more precise details:

To all shipping in the Baltic: In consequence of the capitulation all naval and security forces, as well as commercial vessels, must have left the ports of Courland and Hela by midnight May 8. Transport of German population from the east must be executed with all possible speed. Supreme Naval Command.

Now everyone knew what time remained to him—two whole days. . . . The Russians would arrive punctually at midnight on May 8 and occupy the harbors. Anyone not fortunate enough to have made his escape by then would fall into their hands.

However, things were going to turn out differently.

In the Courland port of Lepaya the 9th Salvage Division assembled all the vessels which could possibly be used for transport purposes. There were mine sweepers and mine layers, patrol boats and fishing cutters, gun carriers, ferryboats, harbor tugs, lighters, and schooners. . . . The responsible officers endeavored to group together all the available craft into something like the usual convoy elements. Far too many vessels, however, were below requirements in speed and quite unseaworthy. If they were left to themselves they would certainly, in the course of their long voyage, either fall a prey to the sea or to the Russians, who would doubtless be waiting to attack. Still, within a convoy, in which the strongest and swiftest have to adapt themselves to the weakest and slowest, the latter would not be entirely left behind and in case of need might count on the others' support.

The very next days confirmed the correctness of this. The Baltic had no intention of fulfilling the soldiers' hopes of a calm sea untroubled by winds and swell. Nor had the Russians any intention of stopping their onslaughts on the innumerable westward-sailing boats which—even after May 9—they still went on attacking both from sky and sea to get them to return to port.

In the meantime all vessels lying in Lepaya and Ventspils announced the very highest number of soldiers which they could accommodate, and on the evening of May 7 the sum total was passed on by a branch of the 9th Salvage Division to the Courland Army Group. The troops in question had to be at the harbor by the afternoon of May 8 to board the boats immediately. The process of shipping was sure to be somewhat prolonged. Nevertheless there was no time to lose; by midnight the ships must all have left the harbors, as any moment after that the Russians might appear.

So the forenoon of the last day of the war passed in feverish preparations. The crews destroyed and threw overboard all that was not urgently necessary for the last trip. Space for their comrades was their watchword. As they collected water and provisions and were being directed to the collecting points in the harbor a severe Russian air raid was going on over Lepaya. The enemy had not been slow to note the Germans' intentions, and was now attempting to frustrate their preparations for flight by means of bombing and naval gunfire. The command bunker, where all the communication wires met, had a direct hit on its concrete cover—fortunately a yard thick; and another bomb burst at the entrance to the bunker, ripping down most of the telephone wires.

It was only a little while prior to this that a communication had come over these same wires from the Army Group saying that certain sections could not arrive before 10:00 P.M.; it was impossible to get them away from their positions earlier. But the naval officers had promised that, if at all possible, a few boats would be detained and accommodation kept on them for these late-comers.

But now a report came in which upset every plan and made the success of the whole convoy scheme more than doubtful.

Those in the command bunker were still dazed after their direct hit when the partition separating them from the next room was pushed aside and a radio operator entered.

"Important radio message, sir," he said, turning to the senior officer present, who took the paper and scanned its significant contents:

Courland Army Group reports Marshal Goworod agrees armistice to begin May 8, 14:00 hours. Inform troops at once. Show white flags in positions. Commander in Chief expects loyal execution as future of all ranks in Courland depends decisively on this. Naval Commander Latvia.

The wireless message was passed from hand to hand.

"Does that mean that the Russians will be entering Lepaya at 14:00 hours?"

"That would be in two hours' time, sir. It's just noon now."

Shortly after another message came in:

Naval Commander of opinion that despite earlier armistice shipping times arranged should be observed.

The men shook their heads dubiously. They had been told that with a midnight capitulation they would have to quit there and then, because the Russians would immediately garrison the harbor. Now, with the armistice due to begin in the early afternoon, were the Russians going to wait for ten hours for the ships to give them the slip? It seemed highly improbable.

"They are doing everything they can to stop our departure," the captain observed. "So of course they will be here as soon as possible. Telephone to all collecting points. . . ."

"We no longer have a telephone to the ships, sir."

"Then we must go ourselves. Get moving; every minute's precious."

Things began really happening now. As fast as they could go, the vessels were directed to the collecting points, and the soldiers streaming into the port were bundled unceremoniously on to them until not a square yard of space was left unoccupied. After that the ships assembled in the outer harbor to await the rest.

Possibly over half the vessels had already been loaded in this way when another radio message, at 16:00 hours, confirmed their fears:

Achtung: Russians marching in.

This news spread like wildfire from ship to ship. By radio, semaphore, and morse every commander was pretty soon aware of what was at stake:

Russians marching in. Utmost speed.

The first convoy of loaded vessels was already on the move from the outer harbor and away from the dangerous coast. The officer in command of the operation now went by air-sea rescue vessel from flotilla to flotilla, from one collecting point to another, releasing the boats and making sure that they were really filled to their utmost capacity, directing empty vessels to other points where he had noticed soldiers waiting. Not until 19:00 hours were the outgoing boats fired on directly by the Russian armor.

Now it was only a question of minutes. While shots came from the outer harbor, the inner was still quiet, with its hundreds of soldiers waiting for a ship. The air-sea rescue vessel now sped after the ferryboats which were precipitately proceeding to sea, but all except one of them were loaded to capacity. That one exception, the *MFP 205,* was turned back to the warship canal. There, on the Korallen pier, the waiting German soldiers were still massed as far as the eye could see. The monitor *Nienburg* —still empty—was there too.

It was a gamble, all right. If the Russians in the meantime penetrated as far as the head of the swing bridge, not only would the waiting men be lost, but also the hundreds on board, for it was perfectly simple to control the entrance to the harbor basin from the bridge.

In a minute both flat-bottomed craft were filled to overflowing.

"Another 20 men!" shouted the skipper of the ferry. "More than that and we'd go down."

Twenty crowded on board. The twenty-first was an elderly man. He stood there, his arms hanging limply by his sides. One of the lucky ones who got on board—a young soldier—all at once noticed him, and just as the ferry was casting off her lines, he jumped back to land and urged the older man to take his place. However, whether it was that the latter hesitated or refused outright to accept such a sacrifice, the ferry had already started and in a few seconds even the best of jumpers could not have reached it. So both were left behind.

Suddenly the rescue vessel with the officer in charge of operations on board was once more fussing alongside. This last had been watching the loading of the boats from some distance away.

"Hurry up, come over, you two!" he yelled. "And another two with you. But get a move on!"

The four of them beamed at their comrades as they were helped on board the little boat. They were the last to be embarked from Lepaya. As even this boat was dangerously overloaded, some 20 soldiers were left behind. At another point a group of 50 stared blankly at the rapidly disappearing boats as they managed to escape from the harbor canal without let or hindrance.

A few moments later the Russians were there. They pounced upon two harbor tugs which had not got away in time, and fired at the others with their self-propelled guns, doing no damage.

Meanwhile, with the night's protecting cloak spread over this queer fleet with its decks thronged with packed masses of humanity, the following radio message was sent out by the leading vessel, a mine sweeper:

19 speedboats, 4 motor mine sweepers, Tsingtau, 1 mine sweeper, 3 patrol boats, 5 ammunition carriers, 43 naval fishing cutters and loggers, 3 Siebel ferryboats, 2 riverboats, 3 naval ferryboats, and 8 more auxiliary ships, with some 18,000 all ranks, left Lepaya by 21:00 hours on May 8 for the west.

Again and again the eastward-bound destroyers encountered small craft of all kinds, tightly packed with soldiers and refugees, going in the opposite direction. There were motorboats among them, sailing yachts and wherries—even a big floating crane out of one of the harbors with a number of lifeboats in tow. As the *Theodor Riedel* came past some light wooden rafts, which like all the rest were full to overflowing with people, the destroyer stopped short and kindly hands threw down to the fugitives food, blankets, and cigarettes. Fortunately the Baltic was still very calm so that even rafts would probably reach safety.

Admiral Thiele breathed more freely on the evening of May 5 on Hela when he was told of the arrival of numerous destroyers and other ships. Relief was in sight; the transport of the multitudes could go on. It was now evident that the decision to keep the smaller vessels, coast steamers, ferries, and so on back in Hela had been correct—now they could ferry the people over to the big ships waiting in the roads. They could do that over and over again for many days yet before the final capitulation took place and the Russians put a spoke in their wheel. Thiele would then at the last moment be able to start in his own small craft for the west.

In the meantime people were converging from all sides on the big ships waiting in the anchorage outside. The crews of the destroyers numbered about 300 and their commanders were prepared to take five times that number on board. But who could count all the folk that pushed, climbed, and wormed their way onto the ships? Who could say whether there were not 2000, 2500, or even 3000 on each destroyer?

Among them were detachments of troops; children, picked up in some street or other in East Prussia and brought along; old bodies with six weeks' foot-slogging behind them; young mothers who had endured their worst hours on the icy roads and now carried their newborn babies with them—all human beings whose fears and privations were plainly written on their faces, who were having their first plate of hot soup in weeks, and now that the strain was relaxed were dissolved in tears of joy and gratitude.

Presently even the officers' living quarters were invaded by refugees, and even such parts of the ship as had, only a few days ago, been forbidden territory to the crew, such as the radio office. In the end scarcely a square foot of space was left on board. Crammed with people, the destroyers, torpedo boats, and the rest cautiously set out on their return trip.

"If I knew in which port or on which coast we could land the lot of them, I should feel happier," the commander of the flotilla remarked. "In Copenhagen we shall probably find the English now."

This assumption was confirmed when next evening some of the heavily loaded destroyers arrived off the Danish capital. They were met by an urgent request not to enter the naval harbor, for the port was already full to overflowing with fugitives and soldiers. There was another reason—and a more important one: the English commanding officer, Rear Admiral Holt, who had in the meantime arrived, required, in the course of the surrender negotiations, that no German ship should leave Danish territorial waters.

So the destroyers could neither get rid of their refugees in the overcrowded naval harbor, nor in consequence could they sail out again to bring back further thousands from Hela. Instead they were brought to a halt outside the Danish three-mile limit. They must make their own arrangements as to how—and to whom—they would dispose of their human cargo.

Meanwhile the surrender negotiations were continuing in Copenhagen. Shortly before noon on May 7 a large closed car drove through the streets of the city, which were thronged with sight-seers. When the Danes caught sight of the British Admiralty flag on the hood they waved and cheered. The English flag lieutenant turned with a smile to the German Admiral sitting at the back of the car. This was Vice-Admiral Kreisch, the commander of the destroyers and last commanding officer of a German formation in the Baltic, who was being driven to the hastily prepared headquarters in the Hotel Angleterre to receive the surrender terms.

Presently the two admirals confronted each other. The Englishman had a human understanding of the Germans' untenable position, but he had strict instructions from London to see that enemy ships were handed over to him—nothing more. It was impossible for him to permit any movement of German ships out of Danish waters.

The situation at the moment was becoming catastrophic. Admiral Kreisch had come straight from the last operations of war —the protection of fugitive transports from the islands off the Pomeranian coast. The people were herded on the boats like cattle going to the slaughterhouse. But it was quite out of the question to disembark them in Copenhagen; the ships must proceed to German ports—and at once; with every day the slender and irreplaceable stocks of fuel were diminishing.

"I am sorry," Rear Admiral Holt said. "I am not in a position to grant you permission to leave Danish territorial waters."

Then the German made a last effort:

"If they sailed close to the coast, they could continue in Danish waters as far as the Flensburg Fjord. If the refugees were landed at the copper mills there, opposite Flensburg, they would still be in Denmark."

The Englishman looked up. Doubtless he read the German's thoughts. Once there no one would stop them sailing on to Germany and getting the folk back on land in their home country. If only—yet perhaps it was best so. At least he could give his formal consent.

Less than 24 hours later the ships left the Danish capital. Admiral Holt's supposition was correct—they were making for Germany. Fifteen thousand soldiers and about 30,000 civilians were being spared a great deal of suffering, and would reach home without loss.

When the negotiations, translated for the Germans by a woman interpreter, came to an end, the English Admiral took the German aside and asked him to bring a male interpreter with him next time.

"You see," he added by way of explanation, "it is unpleasant for me to say no so often to a lady."

The destroyer Admiral was smiling as he emerged from the Hotel Angleterre. Now to get on with the job of saving what could be saved.

That same evening a peculiar thing happened. A few of the destroyers which on May 7 had vainly sought some way of landing their eight- or tenfold "crew" suddenly saw ships approaching—empty ships! It is hard to believe that such vessels, not groaning under masses of refugees, still existed. Now they could hand over their own quota of unfortunates to these "miracle" ships. Two destroyers and a torpedo boat, moreover, actually managed to supplement their oil supply from a tanker which literally crossed their path. And all this took place outside territorial waters, in the open sea—there was nothing to prevent these units going to Hela once more now without in the least infringing the English armistice terms.

Just then a radio message was received. In conformity with the victors' terms it was not in code, but even so, only the initiated would have made much of it:

To Curry immediately everything that can be got there by evening of May 8. Admiral destroyers.

The destroyer captains smiled. "Curry" was Admiral Thiele's nickname from his old sailing-ship days. "To Curry" therefore meant—go to Hela and fetch more refugees. And so on the morning of May 8, shortly after daybreak, they at once set their course for the east again.

Karl Galster, Z 25, and *T 33* were the last vessels to transport soldiers and civilians from the peninsula, when all thought of such action had been given up.

Just before midnight, when they were fully loaded and just weighing anchor, they were ordered by radio to proceed to a Russian-occupied port, and would have obeyed if another such message had not shortly followed the first and contradicted it. This one said:

To all destroyers and torpedo boats. Beware misleading radio messages. Original orders of Grossadmiral to transport people and destroy or sink nothing still remain in force. Keep the peace. Admiral destroyers.

They knew this *"keep the peace"*—it was a genuine message. The officers breathed again and gave orders to sail westward.

At dawn on May 9 numerous small boats which had left

Lepaya and Ventspils and Hela the night before were making very slow headway on their voyage to the west. The people crammed on their decks had had a cold, sleepless night. The wind had freshened and the sea was becoming rougher from hour to hour, so that the river- and ferryboats, none too seaworthy at the best of times, fared specially ill. On top of that there was the conviction, shared by all the soldiers, that the moment it was light enough, the Russian "dance" would start again. Just as they were leaving Ventspils and Lepaya the night before Russian fighters and fighter-bombers had pounced on the small convoys and made several hits. In the meantime, of course, the armistice had come into force for the Soviet Union also. Would they still attempt to halt the transport to the west?

They would soon know the answer to this. With the first light of the new day isolated convoys were picked up by Soviet reconnaisance aircraft—and then, at six in the morning, the attack came with 25 Bostons and IL-2's. Ahead, astern, and alongside the German boats the Russian bombs splashed into the water, but they got no hits this time. Then, as at a word of command, all the light antiaircraft weapons available fired their sheaves of projectiles at the Russian airmen—who withdrew in great haste. Twice more in the next few hours other Russian formations tried their luck before they finally realized that no serious damage could be done to the convoys from the air. They had attacked in spite of the fact that there had been an armistice between Germany and Russia for the last six hours.

There was another and much more formidable foe: the sea. With a strong wind from the southeast and the sea getting up many of the small vessels were in serious difficulties. Parts of the convoy had to halt several times, because the small boats were unable to keep up with the others. In some cases the boats capsized and their occupants had to be taken over by the rest, while others, incapable of making headway alone, had to be taken in tow—all of which, of course, delayed the main convoy considerably.

Then, at five in the afternoon of May 9, when Bornholm had

been passed and most people began to feel that they were already in safety, the lookout man on the *Rugat,* the leading ship of the 9th Salvage Division, suddenly reported three bow waves astern and overtaking rapidly. The men on bridge watch anxiously turned their glasses in the direction indicated. At the same moment the alarm bells rang out:

Russian M.T.B.'s!

They sped past a few hundred yards off the convoy, then sent a spurt of machine-gun bullets across the *Rugat's* bows. That was clear enough. In the leading German ship the engine-room telegraphs were put to "stop," while two German motor mine sweepers turned at an angle of 90 degrees and broke away, seeking safety in flight. They were defenseless, because, like most other boats, they had put their guns out of action as soon as the capitulation came into force. On the *Rugat,* too, only one 8.8-cm. gun was still functioning; all the others had been thrown overboard.

The Russians did not bother about the mine sweepers, but concentrated on the leading German ship, making the international signal to stop. The German seamen and the 1300 or so passengers held their breath.

The radio operator had never prepared a message so quickly as this one. It said:

To 9th Salvage Division. Russian M.T.B.'s coming alongside. What must I do? Rugat.

The Admiral, also still at sea, was only waiting for this. The numerous Russian air attacks long after the armistice came into force had induced him to inquire from Flenburg:

Western convoys being attacked by Russian aircraft. Please say whether armistice canceled. Feel insufficiently informed.

More than likely he did not suppose the armistice to be canceled at all and knew that the Russians simply wanted to stop by any means in their power these ships and soldiers from escaping to the west. The *Rugat* had her reply at once:

Proceed.

Meanwhile one Russian M.T.B. was making its way up to the

Rugat, while the two others from a favorable distance took threatening aim with their tubes. The German ship waited with stopped engines, while the engineers and other seamen stood at their posts in a high state of tension.

Clearly the M.T.B. wanted to come alongside. A Russian sailor was making an effort to throw a line across, but on board the *Rugat* no one made a move to help him. The German soldiers on board were loading their rifles and machine guns—the slightest jolt would set off this general nervous tension and a blood bath follow. The Russians would be the first to suffer on their M.T.B. as it bobbed up and down on the waves only a few yards away, but the Germans would undoubtedly be next —it wouldn't take the other M.T.B.'s a minute to launch their torpedoes.

The *Rugat* was only an old holiday steamer, a "tin Lizzie" which had seen better days in the seaside business between Stettin and Bintz. It had no watertight divisions, and a single hit would send her to the bottom in a few moments.

The two sides stood eying each other. A Soviet officer, wearing a great many decorations, shouted up at the bridge of the German boat:

"Back you all get to Neksö [1]—otherwise you go to kingdom-come!" and he pointed significantly to the torpedoes and other weapons in readiness on board his boat.

On the bridge of the *Rugat* the signal officer of the 9th Salvage Division shouted:

"Come on, Sparks, get this out:

To the 9th Salvage Division. Soviet M.T.B.'s are alongside with torpedoes ready. Question: what are we to do? Rugat.

He had his answer in a minute:

Proceed to point named in instructions. Report current situation. Commander 9th Salvage Division.

All this in uncoded, plain-language text.

The Russians had now moved somewhat astern, obviously with the idea that the Germans would adhere to the new course

---

[1] A small harbor on the Russian-occupied Danish island of Bornholm.

ordered by them. And so they at first did. Then at a given moment they suddenly turned back onto their old course.

"Both engines full speed ahead!" ordered the commander of the *Rugat*. The old ship almost bounced forward, so suddenly did she get under way, the passengers enthusiastically lending the stokers a hand at the boilers.

"Are the 8.8's ready for action?" the commander asked the gunnery personnel. They were. Meanwhile the M.T.B.'s which in their first surprise had remained a fair distance in the offing came up once more, shortly afterward separating in order to overhaul the *Rugat* at larger range on both sides. They had scarcely carried out this maneuver when it was clearly seen from the *Rugat* that they had opened fire, their torpedoes splashing into the water. The passengers flung themselves on the deck. Still steaming at full speed, the ship's helm was put hard over so that she heeled right over to starboard with the passengers, who had never experienced the like, hanging on for dear life. In this way the first two torpedoes were avoided.

The wireless operator had been getting out his message at full speed while all this was going on:

M.T.B.'s attacking with torpedoes. Question: may I open fire?

Before the answer could be received the Russians had begun to fire on the *Rugat* with their quick-firing weapons. Then at last the 8.8-cm. anti-U boat gun on the German ship was given permission to fire. For the first time, close to the leading Russian, a fountain of water rose high in the air.

It was about 8:00 P.M. on May 9, 1945, almost a whole day after the capitulation, that this last naval battle of the war began. But it lasted only a few minutes. With one of the very first shots the Germans got a direct hit on the first M.T.B., which disappeared in a cloud of smoke and steam. Then suddenly there were only two enemy boats and they withdrew at once, firing as they went. Two more torpedoes set out on their blazing path to the *Rugat,* but the German ship's avoiding action was again successful. And that was how this battle ended.

As the mine sweepers slowly made their way back to their

leader and the men were wiping the sweat from their brows, one more message came in from the Admiral Easten Baltic:

If detained by Russians inform them that the ship is on way to west in conformity with agreement between Western Allies and Soviet Supreme Command.

The *Rugat's* officers looked at each other abashed.

"Would they have been likely to believe that?"

At noon the following day the *Rugat*, with innumerable other vessels, was at anchor in the bay outside Kiel.

16

The New U Boats

In spring, 1945, the second world war was making long strides toward its finish. Whatever new weapons the Germans might develop and even get under construction, our whole military effort had received too great a shock for us to be able much longer to postpone the decision. For all that, Field Marshal Montgomery was making a supreme bid to reach the German harbors and dockyards as quickly as possible. For months past the British had noted with increasing anxiety the trickle of information reaching them through various channels on the capacity of these yards—it was U boats they were building, nothing but U boats. And these were not old types, like the ones which had wreaked so much damage on British merchant shipping during 1941 and 1942 and had subsequently, from "black May," 1943, on, had their fangs drawn by radar and from hunters themselves become the prey. No, these new U boats, of which in March, 1945, 100 were already afloat and involved in training, while other hundreds were awaiting their finishing touches in the yards, even outwardly differed enormously from the U boat's traditional lines. What kind of a "comeback" was the German Navy preparing, what answer to the Allies' radar?

Back in May, 1943, Grossadmiral Dönitz had held a meeting in Berlin with scientists and high-frequency technicians to discuss the outstanding efficacy of the Allied anti-U boat measures, and told them some home truths. For radar, that radio detection apparatus which made the invisible visible to the English and Americans, had for sole final effect that of making their ever-growing mass of aircraft and defensive weapons all the sooner aware of the lurking U boats which they could thus surprise and destroy more speedily than ever. Radar, in fact, was the dot on the *i* of the Allied anti-U boat campaign.

"Give us a safeguard," Dönitz asked the technicians; and this they did in fact produce, soon after the secret of the radar invention, its wavelength, and its method of working had been discovered. But it was not in itself decisive—all it could do was to make the German boats aware that they had been spotted by the enemy in time enough to allow them to dive down into the depths of the sea and seek protection there from bombs and depth charges.

But the U boat arm was robbed of its sting by this very fact that the boats were perpetually obliged to dive to escape total destruction. For there, under the water, they were slow, blind, and clumsy. Theoretically the electric motors, battery-driven, gave a top speed of seven knots—but only for one hour; after that the batteries were exhausted. In reality, reduced as it was by the many external projections, the speed amounted only to five knots. Even this speed no commander could venture to keep up for any length of time, for his engine would have exhausted its power after an hour. He was thus forced to maneuver at reduced speed—at two, three, or, at most, four knots. This scarcely gave him an opportunity of pressing home an attack on enemy vessels, unless by chance he met one steaming toward him. For even an escorted convoy, which had always to accommodate its speed of advance to that of the slowest ship, could do from seven to ten knots.

Strange as it may sound, the submarine as hitherto designed was incorrectly named. It was a boat constructed chiefly for operating on the surface, and only in case of an emergency would it dive. Yet that was precisely what they were now being constantly driven to do.

Of course this development had for months been casting its shadow before. Dönitz and his staff were not unduly surprised by the "black May," when 43 U boats were sunk at a blow. For just as they had been making every effort to throw more and more effective U boats into the Battle of the Atlantic, so the enemy had put out every effort to avert the danger.

At the end of November, 1942, the OKM had sent three naval constructors to Dönitz in Paris.

"We must not look at our successes only," the U boat Admiral emphasized. "Look at this list of our losses. Throughout 1940 we lost 24 boats, throughout 1941, 33. In the first half of 1942 the losses kept fairly within bounds, taking into consideration that we were constantly sending fresh ones to the operational areas. But then just have a look how the graph leaps up."

The new figures of losses to which the Admiral pointed were: July, 1942—nine boats; August—12 boats; September—nine boats; October—14 boats, and so far in November another 14.

"And 80 per cent of those losses were on the surface," he went on. "Our U boats are no U boats at all—you know that as well as I do. But they will have to be in the future. I can hardly wait for the development of our new Walter boats."

"What would you think, sir," inquired one of the constructors, "of our building a much larger boat with very strong batteries and a good streamlined form, dispensing with special qualities of seaworthiness on the surface?"

"Fine. But the main thing is that the boats should not have to come to the surface so often, and that they should maintain an underwater speed at which they can operate effectively."

"We'll set about getting the plans ready at once."

"And when can I count on having them?"

"I think in the spring of 1943, sir."

When the first crude and by no means completed plans were submitted to Dönitz in June, 1943, the fears expressed by the Admiral six months previously had been far exceeded; the U boat war had collapsed and the Allied defense got the upper hand.

It was all the more urgent, therefore, to push on with the building of the new boats, Type XXI, as they were called. They were to have three times the number of batteries usual hitherto; their conning-tower superstructure was to be limited to the absolutely necessary, and their hull form to be streamlined. The new type was to have a speed of 17 knots under water—which was almost inconceivable in the circumstances then prevailing. It was really going to be, for the first time, an "undersea boat."

But these were plans only. Not a single order had been placed, nor hammer stroke fallen. The shipbuilders reckoned that the first boats might be ready in a year and a half—or at the end of 1944. And what was going to happen in the meantime?

Dönitz, who had meanwhile become Chief of Naval Staff, was faced with an extremely heavy decision. Should he call off the U boat war and simply scrap his boats now that from one year to another their effectiveness had been so outstripped? The terrible losses suffered had already obliged him to recall commanders from the most dangerous mid-Atlantic areas, which meant that convoys could now travel unhindered between America and Britain, and that U boats must put up with operations in other areas certainly less strongly patrolled but also less important.

Day and night the chief worried over ways in which he could better things for his men. Certainly it was not lightheartedly that he sent them into the unequal fight. The fate of each individual boat represented a personal anxiety to him, and his staff were well aware that no greater joy could be given him than the news that such-and-such a boat that for days had been given up for lost had again signaled from somewhere out at sea. All the same, he had to go on sending them out again—he could not save them up for better times. Every sinking of an enemy ship was important, even though it might no longer be so decisive as had once been hoped. It forced the Allies to keep their defense system in operation, to keep thousands of aircraft searching for U boats, which might otherwise be bombing Germany. And there was another reason: if he were to let his U boats rust in harbor the crews would soon lose their preparedness and never be able to make the "comeback" which he and his officers hoped of the new Type XXI.

But meanwhile elsewhere other people were not sitting idle, waiting submissively for Type XXI to be gotten ready.

Accordingly, radar search receivers were built in so that the boats could know when they were caught in the enemy's radar. The Snorkel, a device for conveying the necessary air to the diesel engines even when traveling under water, was also incorporated. This air mast, the top of which protruded right out of the water, allowed the boat to charge its electric batteries with the diesel without having to surface.

Finally, the obsolete U boat guns were to be replaced by anti-aircraft weapons. If boats were unable to dive away from the sudden attacks of enemy aircraft, they were at least to have a weapon against them. In the ensuing months many a British aircraft was to be shot down by a U boat, though it was much more frequent for the shoe to be on the other foot.

As the air raiders ventured constantly nearer the German U boat "nests" on the French coast, destroying the boats as they crossed the Bay of Biscay, U boats were equipped as "flak traps." They were to lure the aircraft on and, crowded as they now were with antiaircraft weapons, to let it come to a gun battle.

Kapitänleutnant Hartmann was the first to go to sea with his "flak boat," but he was met by a large force of British fighter-bombers and was severely shot up. Everyone standing on the upper deck or superstructure was killed or badly wounded. The commander and all the officers were killed and it was the ship's doctor who eventually managed to bring the boat back to port.

But scarcely was she back at her base and the number of dead and wounded made known than a like number of men from the U boat reserve stormed the depots to take the places of their fallen comrades. This is only one example out of many to show that the fighting spirit of the U boat men was unbroken even in the time of highest losses.

Meanwhile numerous German shipyards were adapting themselves to the new building program. Herr Speer, the minister responsible for the execution of this program, promised that the first new U boat would be ready in May, 1944. Mass production would not come into force until August or September. From that time forward, first ten, then 15, then 20 boats would be finished every month. But constant Allied air attacks held up the program.

At the beginning of 1945 the Allies were preparing for the last onslaught upon Germany from east, west, and south. U boat bases in France had to be given up, and the boats withdrawn to German, Danish, and Norwegian ports, with Scandinavia as point of departure. As every day the enemy crept nearer, the U boat training divisions had also to give up one point after another in the Baltic, first Pillau, then Danzig and Gotenhaven. Despite this they went on training with the new boats—now coming in large numbers from the yards—against the eleventh hour when they too would have a part to play, although German base line was shrinking all the time.

On one of the last days of April, 1945, shortly before the unconditional surrender, *U 2511* went to sea from the Norwegian port of Bergen. She moved out slowly from the lines of her sister ships and gradually gathered speed. The great moment had come. For the first time a new German U boat of Type XXI was about to face the foe. The men on board had a thorough knowledge of her and could depend on her both for cruising and for diving. In a few days now she would be up against the enemy and would show whether she kept her promises or not.

U 2511 had rather an uncertain air in the rough sea; it looked almost as if she were suffering from stage fright before her trial trip.

Korvettenkapitän Schnee, in command of her, was an old hand in U boats. He had seen 17 battles and sunk 200,000 gross tons of shipping. Since the beginning of 1943 he had held an appointment in the shipbuilding commission and had carefully followed every phase in the construction of boats of the XXI type. The same might be said of Fregattenkapitän Suhren, who was now sailing with him in the *U 2511* as chief engineer. Few knew the boat as well as these two did. That was also the reason why Dönitz sent two commanders on operations in one U boat, which was unusual, to say the least. But they were the most suited to handle the boat in any real danger, and their experiences, once they returned home, would be of profit to other new boats.

Scarcely had the escorting patrol vessel which accompanied *U 2511* left her at the limit of her own coastal waters, when the commander gave the order to dive. It was not comfortable enough for him on the surface. He intended to proceed all the way to the Atlantic, under water, at an economical speed.

A very few days later the man at the hydrophones suddenly reported sounds of a propeller. Everybody waited anxiously.

Commander Schnee first went to periscope depth and carefully adjusted his "eye." He saw them, too—a whole line of motor fishing vessels and trawlers, such as the English used here, in the neighborhood of their own coast, for hunting U boats. At the same time a man in the boat below shouted:

"Detection!"

The English had picked up the German U boat; they had spotted it with their Asdic (supersonic detection device). This instrument, developed after the First World War, could determine the presence of submerged U boats by means of scarcely audible sound waves, although it was by no means so perfect as radar and could give accurate results only at short ranges. All the same Asdic, together with hydrophones, is the only means of detecting submerged submarines.

Through the periscope of *U 2511* the commander made sure with a hasty glance that the trawlers were actually approaching him with "white mustaches on their bows," that is to say, at high speed. From his own experience he knew that now there would have been a life-and-death struggle if they had been in one of the old U boats. He could then only have dived and then blindly and gropingly made off in some direction or other— with a top speed of five knots—and for a single hour only. The

Englishmen above could easily have kept up with such a speed. And then would come the "hedgehogs"—whole salvos of depth charges which, dropped together in this way, could do ten or 15 times more damage than a single charge because of the wide area they covered.

They had been doing this with the Germans now for two years. In 1943, 231 U boats were destroyed; in 1944 another 204. For the last two years the Allies had been in full command of the sea again and all the time the U boats had been no more than hunted wild beasts. Now what was going to happen?

Schnee glanced at his first lieutenant.

"We'd like to have a try, wouldn't we?"

"You will attack, sir?"

"No, my lad; we mustn't waste our torpedoes. Our orders are to pick a really big convoy in the West Atlantic."

The periscope was lowered. *U 2511* altered her course and dived deeper in the water—no haphazard operation now, for they were no longer blind under the sea. It was now possible to follow the movements of the enemy overhead: his maneuvers and the course he would now take. The new U boats were no longer dependent on their optical eye, the periscope, but had an electric eye to supplement it.

This was the S gear, which worked in a similar way to the British Asdic. At regular intervals it sent out a solitary *tick* which, radiated through the water, was reflected by the enemy ships and in the fraction of a second marked the corresponding echoes on the U boat's dial indicating the ships, their bearing, and their range. The echoes were transferred to a plot which at the same time automatically marked the U boat's course and speed. After a minute or two came the next *tick*. Again the echoes were transferred and plotted with reference to the previous result. An exact picture was thus obtained of how the enemy was maneuvering in relation to one's own position.

In this case the commander had a perfectly clear picture; there was no blind fumbling this time. He altered his own course and speed exactly in conformity with what the Englishmen above were doing. Should the enemy approach too near, then he would simply give them the slip by putting on speed—eight, 12, 16 knots, exactly as the situation required.

Here it was unnecessary even to increase speed. The trawlers soon gave up wrestling with the choppy sea, while *U 2511*, with her streamlined form, and in 20 fathoms of water, quietly went her way. Soon the Englishmen were left so far behind that the S gear no longer recorded echoes. For a little while longer the sounds of the propellers could still be heard in the hydrophones before they too died away.

Exactly four days passed after that first encounter with the enemy, during which time *U 2511* did not surface once.

Then there was a second report of propeller noises. As the S gear gave no indication, the ships which had been heard must have been pretty far away. The commander gave orders to bring the boat from her present position 40 fathoms under water up to periscope depth. Cautiously his raised his periscope.

What he saw took his breath away. Ahead of them, on the port side, a group of warships was approaching: a British cruiser, screened ahead and on both sides by three destroyers. They were proceeding at medium speed and *U 2511* was so favorably placed in regard to them that only a slight alteration of course would be required to bring her right up to them.

Schnee informed his crew of this situation—it was something they had to experience with him. Then:

"Action stations!"

They rehearsed the attack as if instead of having before them a British cruiser and three destroyers they had still been training in the Baltic and using an old ship for a target. In less than a minute the U boat was once more down to a depth of 40 fathoms. Now the electric eye, the S gear, came into use. Four, even five, *ticks* were sent out; more would have betrayed them. But these four were enough; they gave an accurate picture of the cruiser's course on the plot.

"If they don't alter course we can get to our firing position with silent speed," said the first officer of the watch.

There was nothing to indicate that the English had noticed the U boat; if so, the destroyers would have turned around and attacked, but they did no such thing.

By now *U 2511* was really close, with propeller sounds droning in the hydrophones. *U 2511* dived under the destroyer escorting the cruiser somewhat to starboard, and was still not detected.

After this successful operation Schnee felt able to go up to periscope depth again. He had the cruiser so close in front of him now he could almost touch her—first the bows, then the forward decks and the gun turrets.

"There, have a look at her," Schnee said, stepping back from the sights. Next Suhren took a look through the periscope. Then the first officer of the watch, Kapitänleutnant Lüders. And after him two or three seamen.

Looking at each other, they shook their heads.

"This is my seventeenth operation," Schnee said, "yet I've never had a cruiser in front of my tubes. It just would be now one would turn up."

"I can't help thinking of the past," said Suhren. "Can you imagine our approaching a cruiser without its detecting us, without the destroyers having driven us off?"

"They just didn't hear us," someone remarked. "Just didn't hear us."

As a matter of fact, one could not hear *U 2511*. She was moving so silently that even in the boat itself there was no sound of an engine. The Type XXI U boat has a silent motor which drives the cylinders with a system of soundlessly working belts. Moreover, the propellers are so accurately designed that they cause no unusual disturbance in the water at the number of revolutions required for silent speed. Propeller noises had ceased for this reason. No sound escaped into the outer world to be caught in the highly sensitive enemy listening gear.

With this silent and secret progress the boat attained a speed of five knots, as much as the old boats used to do when exerting full power. But what no commander of those days could have ventured to do, because his battery would have been empty in an hour, offers Type XXI no difficulties. In practice the new boats can remain several days under water without charging their batteries if they cruise at silent speed.

If suddenly there is a hammering note, the engine is switched off and the main electric motors connected. Then the first real underwater boat can show that it possesses power also. It can do 17 knots under water for a full hour, 15 knots over four hours, and 12 knots over ten hours.

Meanwhile, the officers of *U 2511* had been in the conning tower, studying the British cruiser.

Why did *U 2511* not fire torpedoes? The big boat—of 1,621 tons—had six torpedo tubes, all trained forward, and 20 torpedoes on board. There were six live torpedoes in the tubes, which could be fired within 20 seconds. The next six were ready waiting in a quick-loading device.

But still the commander gave no order to fire.

It was in any case unwise of him to remain here between cruiser and destroyers at periscope depth. His boat could fire her torpedoes quite as well at a depth of 25 fathoms. The S gear would give him the mathematically accurate data for it. All that was needed was to send out three *ticks* at intervals of a minute, join up the echoes on the plot, and aim the torpedoes on where the next echo was due to appear. During their Baltic Sea training practice it was said that the result of such methods of operation was always 100 per cent hits.

Then there is firing by plan. Because of its adequate underwater speed the Type XXI boat can always place itself exactly beneath the group of enemy shipping, whether it be a convoy or, as in this case, a group of warships. The S gear will show the commander each time how his own boat lies in regard to the enemy ships. On the same course and at the same speed he moves with—and beneath—the convoy. No one drops depth charges, and there is very little likelihood of the enemy Asdic picking up a single U boat among so many ships' hulls.

And now come the torpedoes. Either the ordinary, aimed torpedo, or the "Lut" or "Fat" torpedoes which first run straight ahead for a short distance, then turn and come back again, turn again, or go on zigzagging until they have hit a ship. Then again there is the *Zaunkönig* (Wren), an acoustic torpedo which is designed to respond to the sounds of the destroyers' propellers. It is difficult for the destroyers to avoid this, and they can only do so by going at full speed, because the Wren is a bit slow. There is, too, the improved Wren, the T11 torpedo, which is not only responsive to destroyers, but homes on ordinary ships as well and is not to be diverted from its course by noise-making devices. In planned attacks six torpedoes are fired simultaneously; they separate fanwise, three to port and three to starboard. After a lapse of time, previously determined, they begin to zigzag and then keep crisscrossing the convoy, although maintaining an equal speed of advance with it.

At that moment all this was going through the heads of the men in *U 2511*. Their boat had not been detected. The superior speed of the British warships had meanwhile left her behind, so that the chance of firing a torpedo was past. No order had been given and no hand raised to fire the live torpedoes at the cruiser.

The commander nodded once more to the others before withdrawing to his cabin to enter the necessary notes in his log.

It was May 7, 1945.

Schnee turned back a few pages to look again at what he had entered two days before:

"5th May, 0300 hours. First radio message.

As from May 5, 0800 hours, cease fire. For U boats at sea attacks forbidden. Break off immediately pursuit of enemy. Return to Norwegian harbors. C.-in-C. U boats.

So *U 2511* never fired. The war, long regarded as hopeless, was now officially at an end.

For this same reason *U 3008*, too, a second new boat of Type XXI, which likewise sailed from Wilhelmshaven on its first operational sortie during the last few days of the war, never fired either. Kapitänleutnant Manseck, its commander, was similarly unable to give the order to fire when he, too, saw British warships cross his torpedo tubes' sights.

The following day *U 2511* came up to the surface again at about the same spot where she had dived a few days before. During the whole trip she had remained under water. But now in Bergen harbor a fresh surprise awaited her.

In the harbor lay a British cruiser, the same one that had been held in the U boat's sights! The German crew all came on deck to have a good look at her—such opportunities did not happen every day—and certainly would not from now on.

"If only they knew their luck!" some of the fellows remarked.

They were to know it soon enough. It was presently heard that a British commission in the cruiser was collecting, on the spot, all particulars concerning the new German U boats. On the very day of the capitulation these Allied officers had been brought by air to Kiel, in order to interview Admiral Godt, Chief of Staff of the C.-in-C. U boats. But all they learned was that so far no particulars were available of the wartime capabilities of the Type XXI boats. They were referred to Bergen.

So here they were, on board the cruiser. The German commander of *U 2511* was also invited to come on board, and Commander Schnee found himself in the presence of an Admiral and high-ranking officers of the Royal Navy. What they wanted to know most of all was how his boat had behaved at sea; how it could be handled; whether he had had any sort of enemy contact.

"Yes," Schnee replied to the last question. "I have."

"And when was that? Which units of the British fleet did you encounter?"

"I encountered the cruiser on which we are now standing."

"That is impossible, sir," said the captain of the cruiser, turning to his Admiral; "we met no German U boats. Neither here on board nor on board the destroyers was anything of the kind detected."

"I know," Schnee smiled. "I had your cruiser within range of my torpedoes, but you did not detect me. I did not fire, for I had already been forbidden to attack on account of our capitulation."

The tension among the officers present resolved itself in a babble of voices, as the British conferred on this information.

"Captain Schnee," said the Admiral, "my officers consider your statement to be impossible. Have you proofs of any sort?"

"Certainly, my logbook. Perhaps you would like to compare the particulars of the encounter with your own log?"

A messenger brought the cruiser's logbook, and a good many pairs of eyes got down to comparing the position entries. There could be no further doubt of it. At the time indicated in the U boat's log, two days before, the British squadron had been at the very point in the North Sea where the Germans claimed to have encountered them. That was indeed a discovery which the majority of people would have thought impossible.

One hundred and twenty of those new electric U boats of Type XXI were ready for service by the beginning of May, 1945, and 86 crews had finished training, but *U 2511* and *U 3008* alone actually sailed on operations against the enemy.

Type XXIII were also electric boats, although of only 232 tons' displacement, much smaller, and intended for coastal operations. Sixty-one of those were in service before the end, and seven took part in hostilities. They all returned safe and sound —five having fired their two torpedoes and gotten hits.

Finally there were eight 280-ton boats ready,[1] of Type XVII, representing the last word in U boat construction. With their "Ingolin" fuel—hydrogen-peroxide—which, with diesel oil and steam, drove the Walter turbine, so-called after its inventor, these boats attained the hitherto-unprecedented speed of 25 knots under water.

But neither could these U boats have affected the course of the war; they were far too late for that.

At the end of May, 1945, Fregattenkapitän Hessler, onetime staff officer for U boat operations, sat on board the former steam-

---

[1] It is believed these boats were still in the experimental stage. [Publishers' note.]

ship *Patria* of the Hapag Line in Flensburg-Mürwik before a British Naval Commission. A captain of the Allied anti-U boat service wanted to know hundreds of details from him.

"And what, in conclusion, is your opinion, Captain Hessler, of the chances your Type XXI boats would have had?"

The German reflected for a minute before he made his reply.

"Perhaps I may refer to what your Prime Minister has said. We had the opportunity to read the summary that Mr. Churchill gave in his broadcast of May 13. If I remember aright, he said: 'The Germans had prepared a new U boat fleet and novel tactics which, though we should have eventually destroyed them, might well have carried the U boat warfare back to the high peak days of 1942.' "

"In my opinion Mr. Churchill was slightly at fault there," the British officer replied. "By comparison 1942 would have been child's play."

In its five and a half years' struggle with an immensely superior enemy the German Navy suffered heavy losses, in spite of which its crews fought on until the moment when their own Commander in Chief was compelled to capitulate. As one of the many nameless who took part in that struggle has said, "We were no heroes. We only did our duty."